SAMS
Teach Yourself
MICROSOFT®
EXCEL 2000

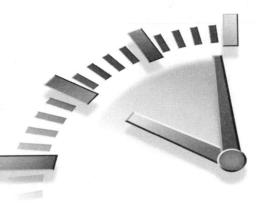

Jennifer Fulton

in 10 Minutes

SAMS

800 East 96th St., Indianapolis, Indiana, 46240 USA

Sams Teach Yourself Microsoft® Excel 2000 in 10 Minutes

To Grandmother Era Fulton. Thank you for your kindness, your love, and most of all, your grandson.

Copyright © 1999 by Sams Publishing

International Standard Book Number: 0-672-31457-6

Library of Congress Catalog Card Number: 98-87211

Printed in the United States of America

First Printing: May 1999

05   04   9   8   7

Bulk Sales

Sams Publishing offers excellent discounts on this book when ordered in quantity for bulk purchases or special sales. For more information, please contact

U.S. Corporate and Government Sales
1-800-382-3419
corpsales@pearsontechgroup.com

For sales outside of the U.S., please contact

International Sales
international@pearsoned.com

Executive Editor
Angela Wethington

Aquisitions Editor
Stephanie J. McComb

Development Editor
Nicholas Goetz

Managing Editor
Thomas F. Hayes

Technical Editor
Dave Bixler

Project Editor
Linda Seifert

Copy Editor
Maryann Steinhart

Indexer
Angela Williams

Production
Lisa England

Proofreaders
Tricia Sterling
Elise Walter

CONTENTS

TELL US WHAT YOU THINK!

As the reader of this book, *you* are our most important critic and commentator. We value your opinion and want to know what we're doing right, what we could do better, what areas you'd like to see us publish in, and any other words of wisdom you're willing to pass our way.

I welcome your comments. You can email, or write me directly to let me know what you did or didn't like about this book—as well as what we can do to make our books stronger.

Please note that I cannot help you with technical problems related to the topic of this book, and that due to the high volume of mail I receive, I might not be able to reply to every message.

When you write, please be sure to include this book's title and author as well as your name and phone or fax number. I will carefully review your comments and share them with the author and editors who worked on the book.

Email: feedback@samspublishing.com

Mail: Mark Taber
              Sams Publishing
              800 East 96th Street
              Indianapolis, IN 46240 USA

Introduction

Suppose you walked into work this morning and found Excel 2000 sitting on your desk. On the box was a note from your supervisor that said: "We need a budget report for Friday's meeting. Here are the numbers. See what you can do."

So, What *Can* You Do?

Well, you could start by wading through Excel's Help system to find out how to perform a specific task—but that might take a while, and you're running out of time. Anyway, the Help system might tell you more than you really want to know (or nothing at all).

Because you're short on time (and patience), what you really need is a practical guide to Excel, one that tells you exactly how to create and print the worksheets, reports, and graphs you need for Friday's meeting.

Welcome to *Sams Teach Yourself Microsoft Excel 2000 in 10 Minutes*

Because most people (including you) don't have the luxury of sitting down uninterrupted for hours at a time to learn Excel, this book doesn't present material in huge chapters you don't have time to read. Instead, it focuses on the most often-used features, covering them in self-contained lessons designed to take 10 minutes or less to complete.

In addition, this book teaches you how to use Excel without relying on technical jargon. By providing straightforward, easy-to-follow explanations, and numbered steps that tell you which keys to press and which options to select, *Sams Teach Yourself Microsoft Excel 2000 in 10 Minutes* makes learning the program quick and easy.

SO WHY SHOULD YOU USE *SAMS TEACH YOURSELF MICROSOFT EXCEL 2000 IN 10 MINUTES*?

Sams Teach Yourself Microsoft Excel 2000 in 10 Minutes is for people like you who:

- Need to learn Excel quickly

- Feel overwhelmed or intimidated by the complexity of Excel

- Want to learn the tasks necessary to accomplish particular goals

- Want a clear, concise guide to the most important features of Excel 2000

HOW TO USE THIS BOOK

Sams Teach Yourself Microsoft Excel 2000 in 10 Minutes consists of a series of lessons that cover the basic, intermediate, and some advanced features of Excel. If this is your first encounter with Excel 2000, you should probably work through Lessons 1 through 14 *in order*. Those lessons lead you through the process of creating, editing, and saving a worksheet. Subsequent lessons tell you how to use the more advanced features to customize your worksheet, including how to use your worksheet as a database; how to add, create, and print graphs (charts); and how to publish your work on the Internet.

ICONS AND CONVENTIONS USED IN THIS BOOK

The following boxed sidebars have been scattered throughout the book to help you find your way around:

> **Tip** These icons mark shortcuts and hints for using Excel efficiently.

Plain English   These icons draw your attention to definitions of new terms.

Panic Button   These tips denote places where new users often run into trouble.

Upgrade Tip   These boxes help you identify features that are new to Excel 2000 so you can quickly learn to take advantage of the advanced timesaving features of the latest version of Excel. In addition, you'll see some special tips along the way that identify how you can use Excel on the Internet.

The following conventions have been used to clarify the steps you must perform:

- Menu items or other commands you select onscreen appear in colored type.

- Data you need to type appears in **bold**, colored type.

- Command, Field, and Key names appear with the first letter capitalized.

- Onscreen messages appear in **bold**.

ACKNOWLEDGEMENTS

Many thanks to the people at Sams Publishing who have helped me with this project. First, thanks to Jamie Milazzo, Acquisitions Editor, for asking me to write this book. Thanks also to Stephanie McComb, who took over the project and handled it magnificently. Thanks to Nick Goetz, Development Editor, for his help on developing this book. Thanks to Linda Seifert, Project Editor, for keeping the manuscript in great shape. And thanks to all the other people at Sams who helped turn this book around on such an aggressive schedule.

TRADEMARKS

All terms mentioned in this book that are known to be trademarks or service marks have been appropriately capitalized. Sams cannot attest to the accuracy of this information. Use of a term in this book should not be regarded as affecting the validity of any trademark or service mark. Windows 95, Windows 98, Excel, and Toolbar are trademarks of Microsoft Corporation.

LESSON 1
STARTING AND EXITING EXCEL

In this lesson, you'll learn how to start and end a typical Excel work session. In addition, you'll learn about the elements of an Excel window.

STARTING EXCEL

After you installed Excel (as covered in the introduction of this book), the installation program returned you to the desktop. To start Excel from there, follow these steps:

1. Click the Start button, and the Start menu appears.

2. Choose Programs, and the Programs menu appears.

3. Choose Microsoft Excel to start the program.

The Excel opening screen appears (see Figure 1.1), displaying a blank workbook labeled Book1. If this is your first time starting Excel, you'll see the Office Assistant asking if you'd like help. Click Start using Microsoft Excel to begin. Excel is now ready for you to begin creating your workbook.

> **Workbook** An Excel file is called a workbook. Each workbook consists of three worksheets (although you can add or remove worksheets as needed). Each worksheet consists of columns and rows that intersect to form boxes called cells into which you enter data. The tabs at the bottom of the workbook (labeled Sheet1, Sheet2, and so on) allow you to flip through the worksheets in a workbook by clicking them with the mouse.

What's the Office Assistant?   When you first start
Excel, you're greeted by an animated icon called the
Office Assistant. (See Figure 1.1.) If you're upgrading
from Excel 97, you'll notice that he acts a bit differently, as you'll learn in Lesson 6. If you've never seen
the Office Assistant before, well, he's there to offer
help, and he'll continue to pop up from time to time
whenever you encounter new features.

If you installed the Office Shortcut Bar, you can also start Excel by clicking the Excel button on the Programs tab of the Shortcut Bar.

A LOOK AT THE EXCEL SCREEN

As you can see in Figure 1.1, the Excel window contains many common
Windows elements, including a menu bar (from which you select commands), a status bar (which displays the status of the current activity), and
toolbars (which contain buttons and drop-down lists that provide quick
access to common commands and features).

New Menu, Please   You'll notice that the menus in
Excel 2000 act a bit differently from their Windows'
brothers. When you open a menu, the commands displayed on it will vary, depending on which options
you select more often. To display all the available
options on a menu, click the down arrow at the bottom of the menu, and it will expand.

Adaptive Menus and Toolbars?   The menus and toolbars you see in Excel will vary as you use the program
and it gets used to your preferences. For the purposes
of this book, the customizable menus have been
turned off, and will therefore display complete

menus. You, however, should leave this option on, since it results in shorter, easier to use menus.

In addition, you will notice that Figure 1.1 shows the Standard and Formatting toolbars on two lines. *This is not the way the program starts out.* You'll probably want to move your toolbars so they look like the figure, since it's an easier way to work. (See Lesson 4 for help on moving the toolbars.) For consistency, both toolbars will be displayed like this throughout the book.

Selector
Menu bar | Toolbars   Column headings   Formula bar

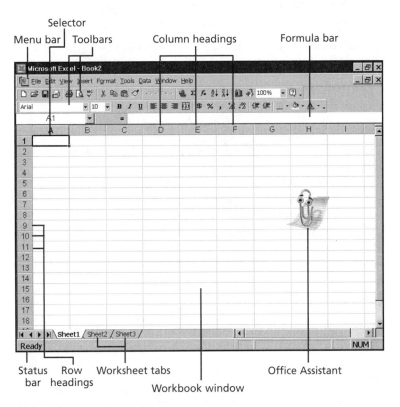

Status Row Worksheet tabs   Office Assistant
bar headings
Workbook window

FIGURE 1.1 Excel's window contains many elements common to other Windows programs.

In addition, the window contains several elements that are unique to Excel, including:

Formula bar. When you enter information into a cell, it appears in the Formula bar. You can use the formula bar to edit the data later. The cell's location also appears in the Formula bar.

Workbook window. Each Excel file is a workbook that initially consists of three worksheets. If needed, you can open several files (workbooks) at a time, each in its own window.

Column headings. The letters across the top of the worksheet, which identify the columns in the worksheet.

Row headings. The numbers down the side of the worksheet, which identify the rows in the worksheet.

Selector. The dark outline that indicates the active cell (the one in which you are working).

Worksheet tabs. These tabs help you move from worksheet to worksheet within the workbook. See Lesson 5 for help.

Cell   Each worksheet in a workbook contains a grid consisting of alphabetized columns and numbered rows. Where a row and column intersect, they form a box called a *cell*. Each cell has an address that consists of the column letter and row number (A1, B3, C4, and so on). You enter data and formulas in the cells to create your worksheets.

EXITING EXCEL

To exit Excel and return to the Windows 98 desktop, perform either of these two steps:

* Open the File menu and select Exit.

  or

* Click the Close (×) button in the upper-right corner of the Excel window.

If you changed the workbook in any way without saving the file, Excel displays a prompt asking if you want to save the file before exiting. Select the desired option. See Lesson 3 for help with saving your workbook.

In this lesson, you learned how to start and exit Excel. You also learned about the elements of the Excel workbook window. In the next lesson, you'll learn how to create and open workbook files.

LESSON 2

CREATING AND OPENING WORKBOOK FILES

In this lesson you will learn how to create new workbooks and open existing workbook files. You will also learn how to locate misplaced files.

When beginning your work in Excel, you have two choices: you can create a new workbook, or you can open an existing one. If you want to create a new workbook, you're probably set, since Excel presents you with a blank workbook each time you open the program. There is another option for starting a new workbook, as you'll learn in a moment. After completing one workbook, you may want to start work on another; at that point, you are once again faced with the same two choices: to start a new workbook, or make changes to one you have already saved.

CREATING A NEW WORKBOOK

When creating a new workbook, you can start with a blank canvas, or you can use a template to create a more complete workbook. A *template* is a predesigned workbook that you can modify to suit your needs. Excel contains templates for creating invoices, expense reports, and other common worksheets.

Here's how you create a new workbook:

1. Open the File menu and select New. The New dialog box appears. As you can see in Figure 2.1, this dialog box contains two tabs: General and Spreadsheet Solutions.

2. To create a blank workbook, click the General tab and click the Workbook icon.

   To create a workbook from a template, click the Spreadsheet Solutions tab. You'll see icons for several common worksheet types. Click the icon for the type of workbook you want to create. If that template has not yet been installed, you'll be prompted to insert the Office 2000 CD. Follow the onscreen instructions.

3. After you've made your selection, click OK or press Enter. A new workbook opens onscreen with a default name in the title bar. Excel numbers its files sequentially. For example, if you already have Book1 open, the Workbook title bar will read Book2.

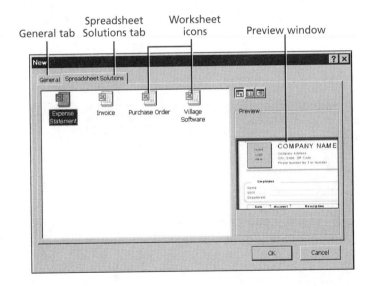

FIGURE 2.1 Click the icon for the type of worksheet you want to create.

> **Instant Workbook** If you want to create a blank
> workbook (instead of creating one from a template),
> you can bypass the New dialog box by clicking the
> New button on the Standard toolbar. Excel opens a
> new workbook window without displaying the New
> dialog box.

OPENING AN EXISTING WORKBOOK

If you have a workbook you've previously saved that you would like to
work on, you must open the file first, before you can make any changes.
Follow these steps to open an existing workbook:

1. Open the File menu and select Open, or click the Open button
   on the Standard toolbar. The Open dialog box shown in Figure
   2.2 appears.

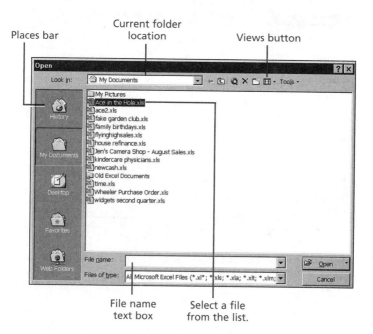

FIGURE 2.2   The Open dialog box.

2. If the file is not located in the current folder, open the Look in drop-down list box and select the correct drive and folder.

   Alternatively, you can switch to several common folders by clicking the appropriate icon on the Places bar:

   History. This folder contains links to as many as 50 of your most recently used documents.

   My Documents. The default folder for your Office programs; you'll probably find most of your documents here.

   Desktop. From here, you can access any folder on your computer.

   Favorites. If you use certain files a lot, you can save them to the Favorites folder, and then quickly open them by clicking this icon.

   Web Folders. This folder contains links to folders on your company's intranet, or on the Internet. You can use this icon to quickly open documents you've published to the Web or to your company's intranet.

3. Select the file you want to open in the files and folders list. Or, type the name of the file in the File name box. (As you type, Excel highlights the first filename in the list that matches your entry; this is a quick way to move through the list.)

Open a Web File   If you know a Web file's location, you can type it in the File name text box, such as `http://www.fakeinternetcompany.com/Sales/Widgets/firstqtr.xls`. If you're not sure of a file's location, you can browse the Web by clicking the Search the Web button.

---

4. To see a preview of the workbook before you open it, click the Views button and select Preview. Excel displays the contents of the workbook in a window to the right of the dialog box.

5. Click Open or press Enter. There are other open options, if you click the arrow on the Open button:

- To open the workbook as a read-only file (to prevent you from accidentally changing data), click the arrow and select Open Read-Only.

- To open a copy of the workbook so that you can create a similar workbook without changing the original, click the arrow and select Open as Copy.

- To open an HTML document in your Web browser instead of within Excel, click the arrow and select Open in Browser.

> **Recently Used Workbooks**　If the workbook you want to open is one of your four most recently used workbooks, you'll find it listed at the bottom of the File menu. Just open the File menu and select it from the list. To open other recently used documents, use the History folder in the Open dialog box.

You can also open a specific workbook when you first start Excel. Just click the Start button on the Windows taskbar and select Open Office Document. Select the workbook you want to open and click Open. Excel starts with the workbook you selected open and ready to edit.

FINDING A WORKBOOK FILE

If you forget where you saved a file, Excel can help you. You can use the Find tool in the Open dialog box to locate your lost file. Here's how:

1. Select File, Open, or click the Open button in the Standard toolbar. The Open dialog box appears (see Figure 2.2).

2. Change to the drive and/or folder you want to search. You can click the Desktop icon in the Places bar and click My Computer to search all the drives on your computer.

3. Click the Tools button and select Find. The Find dialog box appears, as shown in Figure 2.3.

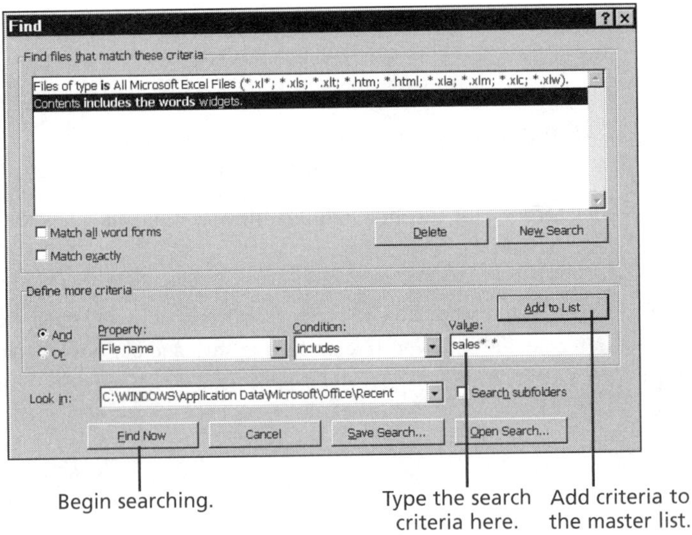

Begin searching.   Type the search   Add criteria to
                                    criteria here.   the master list.

FIGURE 2.3   Find helps you to locate a workbook.

4. Open the Property drop-down list and select the type of item you want to search, such as File name or Contents.

5. Select a Condition, such as Includes.

6. Type a Value to compare, such as First Quarter Sales.xls.

When needed, you can use wildcard characters in place of characters you can't remember. Use an asterisk in place of a group of characters; use a question mark in place of a single character. (For example, if you're searching by filename and you enter sales??, Excel finds all files whose file names begin with the word "sales" followed by two characters, such as SALES01, SALES02, and so on. If you enter sales*, Excel will find all files beginning with the word "sales" followed by any number of characters, such as SALES01, or SALES HISTORY.)

7. To have Excel search all subfolders of the drive you specify, select the Search subfolders option.

8. Click Add to List.

9. If you want to add additional search criteria, choose either the And or the Or option, and then repeat steps 3 to 7.

10. When you finish entering your search criteria, click Find Now. Excel finds the files that match the search instructions you entered and displays them in the files and folders list.

11. Look through the list, highlight the file you want, and click the Open button.

In this lesson, you learned how to create new workbooks and open workbooks. In the next lesson, you'll learn how to save and close workbook files.

Lesson 3

Saving and Closing Workbook Files

In this lesson you will learn how to save workbook files and how to close them when they are no longer needed.

Saving and Naming a Workbook

Whatever you type into a workbook is stored only in your computer's temporary memory. If you exit Excel, that data will be lost. Therefore, it is important to save your workbook files to a disk regularly.

The first time you save a workbook to a disk, you have to name it. Follow these steps to name your workbook:

1. Open the File menu and select Save, or click the Save button on the Standard toolbar. The Save As dialog box appears (see Figure 3.1).

2. Type the name you want to give the workbook in the File name text box. You can use up to 218 characters, including any combination of letters, numbers, and spaces (for example, Fourth Quarter Sales 1998).

3. Normally, Excel saves your workbooks in the My Documents folder. To save the file to a different folder or drive (such as a network drive), select it from the Save in list.

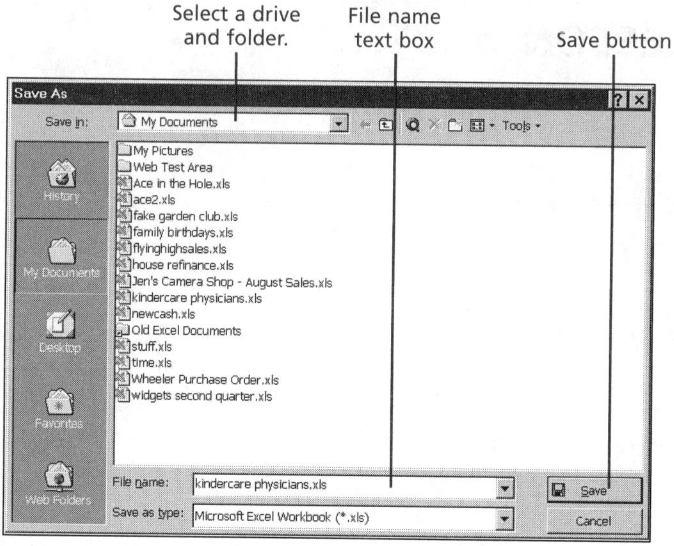

Select a drive
and folder.

File name
text box

Save button

FIGURE 3.1   The Save As dialog box.

> **Default Directory**   Files are typically saved to the My
> Documents directory. You can change the default to
> your own private directory if you want. Open the
> Tools menu, select Options, and click the General tab.
> Click in the Default file location text box and type a
> complete path for the drive and directory you want to
> use (the directory must be an existing one). Click OK.

The Places bar contains icons linking you to other folders in which you
might want to save your file. To change to any of these folders, click the
appropriate icon on the Places bar:

History. This folder contains links to up to 50 of your most
recently used documents. You cannot save a file to this folder.

My Documents. The default folder for your Office programs.

Desktop. From here, you can access any folder on your computer
in which you might want to save your file. If you save a file to the
Desktop folder itself, it's displayed as an icon on the Windows

desktop. Double-click the icon on your desktop to quickly start Excel and open the workbook file at the same time. If you're working on a project in Excel on a daily basis, you might want to have the file icon on the desktop for your convenience.

Favorites. If you use certain files a lot, save them to the Favorites folder.

Web Folders. This folder contains links to folders on your company's intranet, or the Internet. You can use this icon to quickly open documents you've published to the Web or your company's intranet.

The Folder I Want to Save in Doesn't Exist!   No problem—just create it! To create a new folder, click the Create New Folder button on the toolbar of the Save As dialog box, type a name for the new folder, then press Enter.

4. Click the Save button or press Enter.

To save an open file you have saved previously (and named), all you need to do is click the Save button. (Or you can press Ctrl+S or use the File, Save command.) Excel automatically saves the workbook and any changes you entered without displaying the Save As dialog box.

Save a Workspace   After opening several workbooks and arranging them onscreen, you can save the arrangement as a workspace, and use that workspace to quickly reopen and arrange these same workbooks at a later time. To save a workspace, first open the workbooks you want and arrange them onscreen as desired. Then open the File menu and select Save Workspace. Give the arrangement a name and click OK. To open the workspace later on, click the Open button and select Workspaces from the Files of type list.

SAVING A WORKBOOK UNDER A NEW NAME

Sometimes you might want to change a workbook but keep a copy of the original workbook, or you may want to create a new workbook by modifying an existing one. You can do this by saving the workbook under another name or in another folder—the original file remains unchanged, in its original location. The following steps show how you do that:

1. Open the File menu and select Save As. You'll see the Save As dialog box, just as if you were saving the workbook for the first time.

2. To save the workbook under a new name, type the new filename over the existing name in the File name text box.

3. To save the new file on a different drive or in a different folder, select the drive letter or the folder from the Save in list.

4. To save the new file in a different format (such as Lotus 1-2-3 or Quattro Pro), click the Save as type drop-down arrow and select the desired format.

5. Click the Save button or press Enter.

> **Backup Files**   You can have Excel create a backup copy of any workbook file you save. That way, if anything happens to the original file, you can use the backup copy. To turn the backup feature on, click the Tools button in the Save As dialog box, and select General Options. Select Always create backup, and click OK. To use the backup file, choose File, Open to display the Open dialog box, and then select Backup Files from the Files of type list. Double-click the backup file in the files and folders list to open it.

CLOSING WORKBOOKS

When you close a workbook, Excel removes it from the screen. To close a workbook, follow these steps:

1. If the window you want to close isn't currently active, make it active by selecting the workbook from the list of workbooks at the bottom of the Window menu.

You can also display a workbook by clicking its button on the Windows taskbar.

2. Click the Close (×) button in the upper-right corner of the workbook. (There are two Close buttons: the one on top closes Excel; the one below it closes the current workbook window.)

It's Closing Time! If you have more than one workbook open, you can close all of them at once by holding down the Shift key, opening the File menu, and selecting Close All.

In this lesson, you learned how to save workbooks and close them. The next lesson teaches you how to use Excel's toolbars.

LESSON 4

USING EXCEL'S TOOLBARS

In this lesson, you will learn how to use Excel's toolbars to save time when you work. You will also learn how to arrange them for maximum performance.

USING THE TOOLBARS

Excel initially displays only the Standard and Formatting toolbars, as shown in Figure 4.1. The Standard toolbar provides tools (or buttons, if you prefer) for common tasks such as opening, closing, and creating files. The Formatting toolbar provides tools for formatting your worksheet's data and cells.

> **What Is a Toolbar?** An Excel toolbar is a collection of icons (small pictures) displayed in a long bar (or floating window) that can be moved and reshaped to make it more convenient for you to use. Each icon represents a common command or task.

Here's what you need to know about using a toolbar:

- To use a tool from a toolbar, click it.

- Initially, the Standard and Formatting toolbars are displayed in the same row. To select a button that's not currently displayed, click the More Buttons button at the end of each toolbar and then click the toolbar button you want. (You can move the Formatting toolbar to its own row if you want to; see the upcoming section, "Moving Toolbars" for help.)

- To view the name of a tool, position the mouse pointer over it. A ScreenTip appears, displaying the name of the tool (as shown in Figure 4.1).

- To get help with the command associated with a particular tool, select Help, What's This? or press Shift+F1. The mouse pointer changes to a question mark. Move the question mark pointer over a tool and click it. A Help window appears, explaining the tool's use.

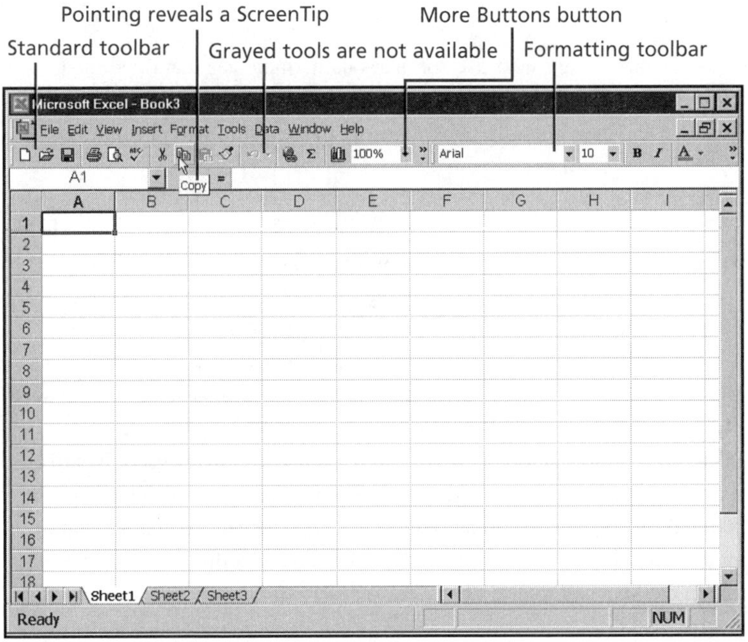

Pointing reveals a ScreenTip   More Buttons button

Standard toolbar | Grayed tools are not available | Formatting toolbar

FIGURE 4.1 The Standard and Formatting toolbars provide quick access to Excel's most commonly used features.

 Off Duty If a tool appears grayed, then it is currently unavailable. Tools become unavailable when they are not applicable to your current activity.

TURNING TOOLBARS ON AND OFF

By default, Excel displays just the Standard and Formatting toolbars. If you find that you don't use these toolbars, you can turn one or both of them off to free up some screen space. In addition, you can turn on other toolbars (although most toolbars appear on their own when you perform a related activity).

Follow these steps to turn a toolbar on or off:

1. Open the View menu and choose Toolbars. A cascading menu appears.

2. A check mark next to a toolbar's name indicates that the toolbar is currently being displayed. To turn a toolbar on or off (whichever it's not), click its name in the list to add or remove the check mark.

> **Quick View**   To display a hidden toolbar quickly, right-click on an existing toolbar and select the toolbar you want to display from the shortcut menu that appears.

Because the Drawing toolbar is a popular toolbar with many users, Microsoft provides an additional way to display it when needed. Just click the Drawing button on the Standard toolbar to turn it on. (If the Standard and Formatting toolbars are sharing the same row, you'll need to click the More Buttons button on the Standard toolbar, then click the Drawing button.)

MOVING TOOLBARS

After you have displayed the toolbars you need, you can position them within the work area where they will be more convenient. For example, you might want to move the Formatting toolbar under the Standard toolbar so you can access all of its buttons easily. Figure 4.2 shows an Excel window with three toolbars in various positions on the screen.

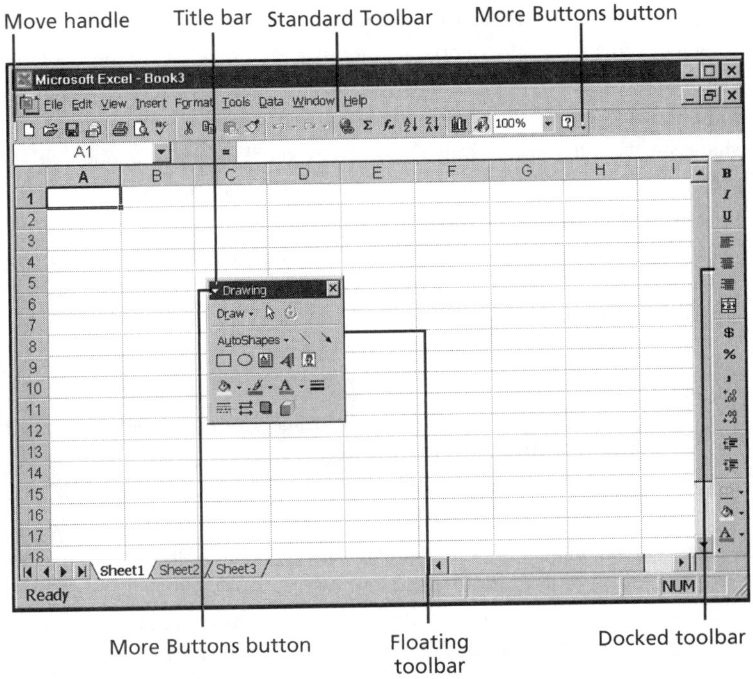

FIGURE 4.2   Three toolbars in various positions.

Here's what you do to move a toolbar:

1. Click a toolbar's move handle. (If the toolbar is floating in the middle of the window, click its title bar instead.)

2. Hold down the mouse button as you drag the toolbar to where you want it. You can drag a toolbar to a side or to the bottom of the window (to a "dock") or let it "float" anywhere in the window.

3. If you float a toolbar in the work area, drag a corner to reshape it as needed.

Floating Toolbar   A *floating toolbar* acts just like a window. You can move a toolbar like a window, and resize it. To do that, position the mouse pointer over the side or bottom of the toolbar, and drag the edge outward or inward to create the desired shape.

If you drag a floating toolbar to a docking area at the top or bottom of the screen, it turns back into a horizontal toolbar. By dragging the toolbar to a side docking area, it will turn into a vertical toolbar. (If you drag it back into the work area at a later time, the toolbar will resume its former shape.) Although you can drag a toolbar anywhere, if you drag one that contains a drop-down list (such as the Standard or Formatting toolbar) to the left or right side of the window, the drop-down list buttons—such as the Font and Font Size buttons—disappear (see Figure 4.2). If you move the toolbar back to the top or bottom of the window (or let it float) the drop-down list buttons reappear.

 Quickly Dock a Toolbar   To quickly dock a floating toolbar, double-click its title bar.

By the way, the menu bar is treated the same as other toolbars. This means you can move it to the side of a window, or you can float it in the middle of the screen if you want. It also means that you can customize the menu bar in a manner similar to toolbars, as discussed in the next section.

CUSTOMIZING THE TOOLBARS

Because you use toolbars often, it makes sense to customize them to the way you work. The most common task you'll want to perform is adding and removing buttons from a toolbar, so that it contains only the tools you really use. Here's how:

1. To add or remove buttons on a toolbar, click More Buttons. (On a floating toolbar, the More Buttons button is the down arrow at the left end of the title bar. (See Figure 4.3.) A cascading menu appears.

2. Click Add or Remove Buttons. Another menu appears.

3. Buttons that already appear on the toolbar have a check mark in front of them. If you click one of these buttons, the check mark disappears, and the button is removed from the toolbar.

   If you click a button that does not have a check mark, then a check mark appears, and the button is added to the toolbar.

Add or Remove   More Buttons
Buttons button   button

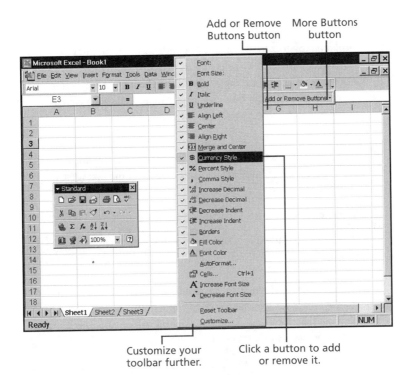

Customize your   Click a button to add
toolbar further.   or remove it.

FIGURE 4.3   Adding and removing buttons from your toolbars is
easy.

Easy as Pie! If you never bothered to customize your
toolbars before, you might want to try now, because
in Excel 2000, it's a whole lot easier!

With the Customize dialog box, you can further customize your toolbars.
To display the Customize dialog box, select Customize from the Add or
Remove Buttons menu in step 2.

On the Toolbars tab, you can:

- Display a toolbar that is not currently visible by selecting it from
  the list.

On the Commands tab, you can perform any of the following:

- Add a button to a toolbar that does not appear on the Add or Remove Buttons list by selecting its category from the Categories list. (For example, to add the Clear Contents button to a toolbar, select the Edit category.) You can add menus to a toolbar as well; you'll find them listed at the bottom of the Categories list.

  After you've selected the proper category, click the command you want in the Commands list, and drag it off the dialog box and onto the toolbar.

- Remove a button from a toolbar by dragging it off the toolbar.

- Rearrange the buttons on a toolbar by dragging them around within the bar.

On the Options tab, you can change options which affect all your Office applications (except for the Standard and Formatting toolbars Share one row option, and the Reset my usage data option, which affect Excel only). Just select whatever options you want.

 I Messed up my Toolbar! To return a toolbar to its default settings (the way it was before you or someone else changed it), select the **Reset Toolbar** command from the **Add or Remove Buttons** menu.

In this lesson, you learned how to use Excel's toolbars and to customize them for your own unique needs, In the next lesson, you'll learn how to get around in Excel.

Lesson 5

Getting Around Excel

In this lesson, you'll learn the basics of moving around in a worksheet and moving within a workbook.

Moving from Worksheet to Worksheet

By default, each workbook starts off with three worksheets. You can add or delete worksheets from the workbook as needed. Because each workbook consists of one or more worksheets, you need a way of moving from worksheet to worksheet easily. Use one of the following methods:

- Click the tab of the worksheet you want to go to (see Figure 5.1). If the tab is not shown, use the tab scroll buttons to bring the tab into view, and then click the tab.

  or

- Press Ctrl+PgDn to move to the next worksheet or Ctrl+PgUp to move to the previous one.

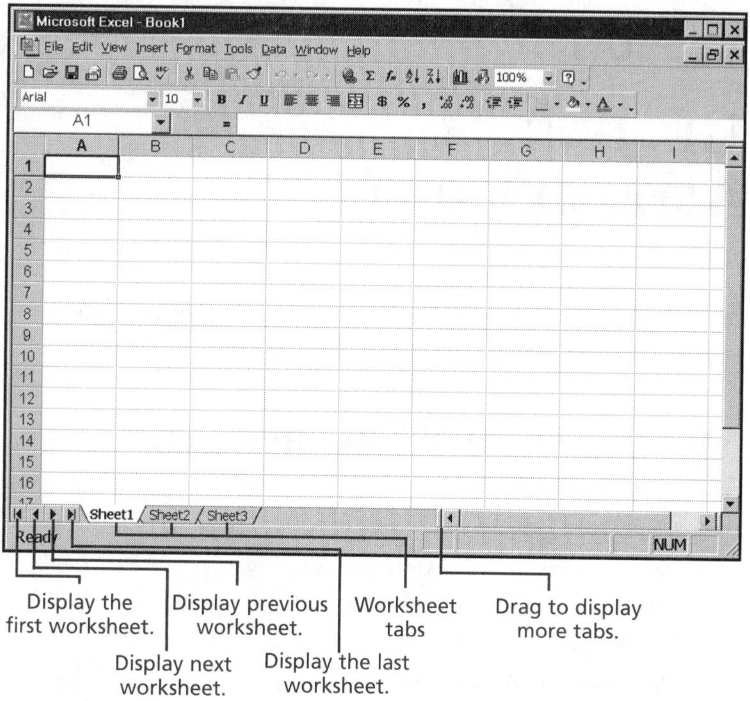

Display the first worksheet.
Display previous worksheet.
Worksheet tabs
Drag to display more tabs.
Display next worksheet.
Display the last worksheet.

FIGURE 5.1   Use the tabs to move from worksheet to worksheet.

MOVING FROM WORKBOOK TO WORKBOOK

Sometimes you may have several workbooks open at a time. (If you need help opening a workbook, see Lesson 2.) When you're working with several workbooks, you often need to switch back and forth to view or edit their contents. There are several ways to do that. Here are two:

- Open the Window menu and select the name of the workbook to which you want to switch.

   or

- Press Ctrl+F6 to move from one workbook window to another.

> **Taskbar Switching**   With Excel 2000, you can now switch between open workbooks like you switch between programs. Each workbook has its own button on the Windows taskbar, as shown in Figure 5.2. To switch between workbooks, click the button for the workbook you want.

Name box

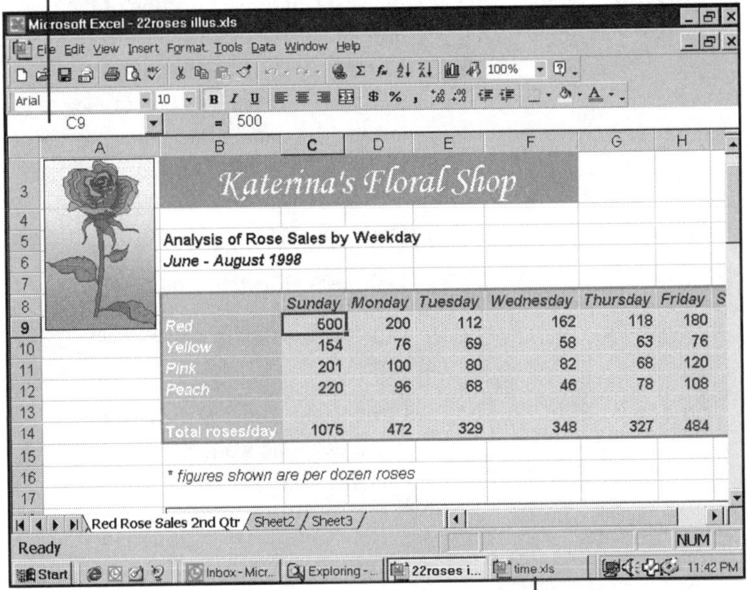

Click the button of the workbook to which you want to switch.

FIGURE 5.2   You can now switch between workbooks using the Windows taskbar.

MOVING WITHIN A WORKSHEET

To enter your worksheet data (which you'll learn to do in Lesson 9), you'll need some way of moving to the various cells within the worksheet. Keep in mind that the part of the worksheet displayed onscreen is only a small piece of the actual worksheet.

USING THE KEYBOARD

To move around the worksheet with your keyboard, use the keys listed in Table 5.1.

TABLE 5.1   MOVING AROUND A WORKSHEET WITH THE KEYBOARD

PRESS THIS...	TO MOVE...
⬆,⬇,⬅,➡	One cell in the direction of the arrow.
Ctrl+⬆, Ctrl+⬇, Ctrl+⬅, Ctrl+➡	If the current cell is blank, moves to the next cell in the direction of the arrow that contains data. If the current cell contains data, moves to the last cell in the direction of the arrow that contains data.
PgUp	Up one screen.
PgDn	Down one screen.
Home	Leftmost cell in a row (column A).
Ctrl+Home	Upper-left corner of a worksheet (cell A1).
Ctrl+End	Lower-right corner of the data area (the area of the worksheet that contains data).

> **Move to a Specific Cell**   To move quickly to a specific cell on a worksheet, type the cell's address in the Name box at the left end of the Formula bar and press Enter (see Figure 5.2). A cell address consists of the column letter and row number that define the location of the cell (for example, C25). To go to a cell on a specific worksheet, type the worksheet's name, an exclamation point, and then the cell address (such as Sheet3!C25) and press Enter.

USING A MOUSE

To scroll through a worksheet with a mouse, follow the techniques listed in Table 5.2.

TABLE 5.2   MOVING AROUND A WORKSHEET WITH THE MOUSE

CLICK THIS...	TO...
Any visible cell	Move the selector to that cell.
Up or down arrows on the vertical scrollbar	View one more row, up or down.
Left or right arrows on the horizontal scrollbar	View one more column, left or right.
The scroll box and drag it	Move through a worksheet quickly. As you drag, a ScreenTip displays the current row/column number.

Size Matters   Keep in mind that the size of the scroll box changes to represent the amount of the total worksheet that is currently visible. So, if the scroll box is large, you know you're seeing almost all of the current worksheet in the window. If the scroll box is small, most of the worksheet is currently hidden from view.

USING THE INTELLIMOUSE

If you use the Microsoft IntelliMouse, you can move through a worksheet even more quickly than you can with a conventional mouse. Here's how:

DO THIS...	TO...
Rotate the wheel in the middle of the mouse forward or back.	Scroll a few rows (scroll up and down)
Click and hold the wheel button, and then drag the mouse in the direction in which you want to pan (scroll quickly). The farther away from the origin mark (the four-headed arrow) you drag the mouse, the faster the panning action. To slow the pan, drag the mouse back toward the origin mark.	Scroll faster (pan)
Click the wheel once, and then move the mouse in the direction in which you want to pan. (You'll continue to pan when you move the mouse until you turn panning off by clicking the wheel again.)	Pan without holding the wheel
Press the Ctrl key as you rotate the middle wheel. If you zoom out, you can click on any cell you wish to jump to. You can then zoom back in so you can see your data.	Zoom in and out

In this lesson, you learned how to move through a worksheet, and to move from workbook to workbook. In the next lesson, you'll learn how to get help in Excel.

LESSON 6

GETTING HELP

In this lesson, you'll learn how to use the Office Assistant and how to navigate the Excel Help system.

You have probably already met the Office Assistant: it's that little paperclip that popped up to give you advice when you started Excel the first time. Don't let Clippit's whimsical appearance fool you, though. Behind him is a very powerful Help system.

ASKING THE OFFICE ASSISTANT FOR HELP

When you need help with something, just ask the Office Assistant:

1. If the Office Assistant is not visible, click the Microsoft Excel Help button on the Standard toolbar, or press F1. If the Assistant is visible but the help bubble is not (see Figure 6.1), click the Office Assistant to display it.

FIGURE 6.1   Office Assistant is at your service.

2. Type a question into the text box. For instance, you might type **How do I print?** or type a keyword such as **printing** to get help on printing your worksheet.

3. Click the Search button or press Enter. Office Assistant displays some topics that might match what you're looking for. For instance, Figure 6.1 shows Office Assistant's answer to the question, "How do I print?"

4. Perform any of the following:

   - Click the topic that best describes what you're trying to do. For instance, you might choose Start a new page by inserting a page break (see Figure 6.1). A Help window appears with instructions for the specified task.

   - If none of the topics describe what you want, click the See more... option at the bottom of the list to view more suggestions. To return to the first list, click the See previous... option.

   - If you still can't locate a topic you want, you can click the None of the above, look for more help on the Web option (that is, if you have a connection to the Internet), or you can type a different question into the text box and press Enter.

5. If you selected a topic in step 4, a Help window appears right next to the Excel window, so you can easily complete the steps for the task in the open workbook. (See Figure 6.2.) If you need help navigating the Help window, see the next section.

6. If you'd like more help, you can ask the Office Assistant another question. Just click on the assistant to display the help bubble again, type your question, and press Enter.

7. When you're through asking questions, you can remove the Help window by clicking its Close button. The Office Assistant remains onscreen. It's programmed to stay out of your way, but if you'd like to "put Clippit to sleep," just right-click on it and select Hide.

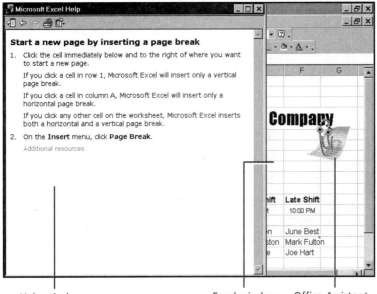

Help window   Excel window   Office Assistant

FIGURE 6.2   The Help window appears next to the Excel window.

NAVIGATING THE HELP WINDOW THAT APPEARS

After selecting a topic from the Office Assistant bubble, a Help window appears. When it does, you can read the information onscreen or do any of the following:

- Click any underlined term (such as the term "data area" in Figure 6.3) to see a definition of it.

- Click any underlined topic to jump to the related Help page.

- Click a >> button to jump to another Help screen. For instance, in Figure 6.3, the >> button will display a screen that explains how to control the order in which formulas are calculated.

- Click the Show Me button (when it's available) to let Excel walk you through the steps for a procedure.

- Return to the previous Help topic you viewed by clicking the Back button. You can click the Back button multiple times.

- Return to your original screen by clicking the Forward button as many times as needed.

- Print a hard copy of the information by clicking the Print button.

- Display the Help tabs so you can look up a topic yourself by clicking the Show button. (See the next section for more information.)

- Close the Help window by clicking the Close (×) button.

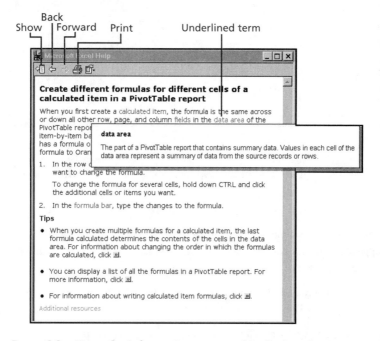

Figure 6.3   Once the information you need is displayed, you can read it, print it, or move on to another Help topic.

HELPING YOURSELF

After using the Office Assistant to try to locate the information you need, you may decide that it'll be easier to browse through Help yourself. It's simple enough to do:

1. Expand the Help window by clicking the Show button at the top of the Help window. (See Figure 6.3.) The Help tabs appear.

2. Click the appropriate tab (Contents, Answer Wizard, or Index) and type the required information to locate the help you need. (See the following sections for help using each tab.)

3. Click the Close button to close Help when you're through.

I Can Do It Myself!   If you prefer to locate information on your own, you can turn off the Office Assistant permanently. Then, when you click the Microsoft Excel Help button, you'll go directly to the Help system, and bypass the assistant altogether. Lesson 7 shows you how.

THE CONTENTS TAB

The Contents tab of Help system is a series of "books" you can open. Each book has one or more Help topics in it, and some books contain subbooks. Figure 6.4 shows a Contents screen.

To select a Help topic from the Contents screen, follow these steps:

1. Click the Contents tab.

2. Find the book that describes, in broad terms, the task you need help with. Double-click the book, and a list of Help topics appears below the book (see Figure 6.4).

3. Click a Help topic to display it. If needed, point to a topic, and a ScreenTip appears, displaying the complete topic name.

4. You can click another Help topic, if needed, to display it instead. When you're through with Help, click the window's Close (×) button to exit.

Closed book

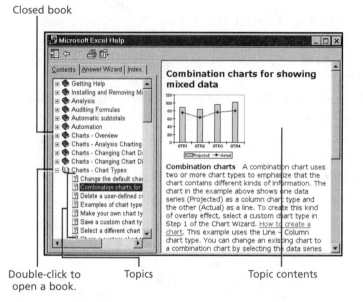

Double-click to   Topics   Topic contents
open a book.

FIGURE 6.4   The Contents screen.

THE ANSWER WIZARD TAB

If you know the exact topic you're searching for, it's easy to locate it using the Contents or Index tabs. However, if you're not exactly sure what something is called, or what topic it might be listed under, ask the Answer Wizard instead. Using the Answer Wizard is similar to asking the Office Assistant for help:

1. Click the Answer Wizard tab.

2. Type your question in the top box, as shown in Figure 6.5.

3. Click Search. A list of topics appears.

4. Browse the topics that appear in the lower box, and click the one you want. The topic appears in the right-hand pane.

5. Click another topic if you like. When you're through with Help, click the window's Close (×) button to exit.

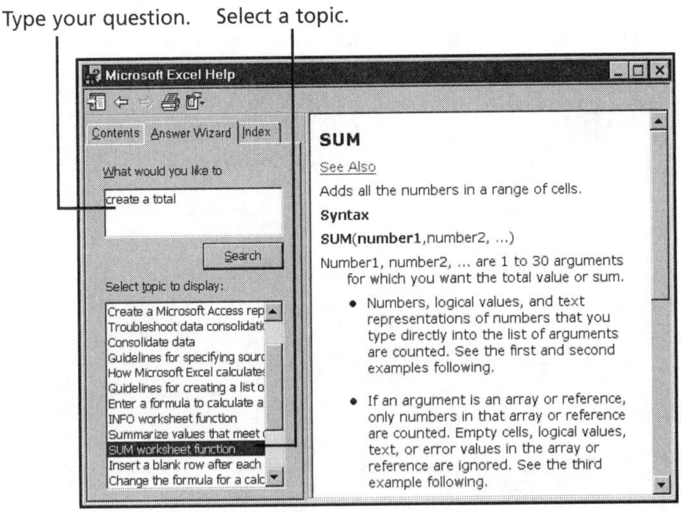

Type your question.   Select a topic.

FIGURE 6.5   Ask the Answer Wizard for help when you need it.

THE INDEX TAB

The Index is an alphabetical listing of key terms found in all the available Help topics. It's like the index to a book. Follow these steps to use the Index:

1. Click the Index tab.

2. Type the keyword for the topic you're looking for in the step 1. Type keywords box, or select the exact keyword you want from the step 2. Or choose keywords list. (See Figure 6.6.)

3. Click Search.

4. Click the topic you want in the step 3. Choose a topic box. The topic appears in the right-hand pane.

5. Double-click another topic if you like. When you're through with Help, click the window's Close (×) button to exit.

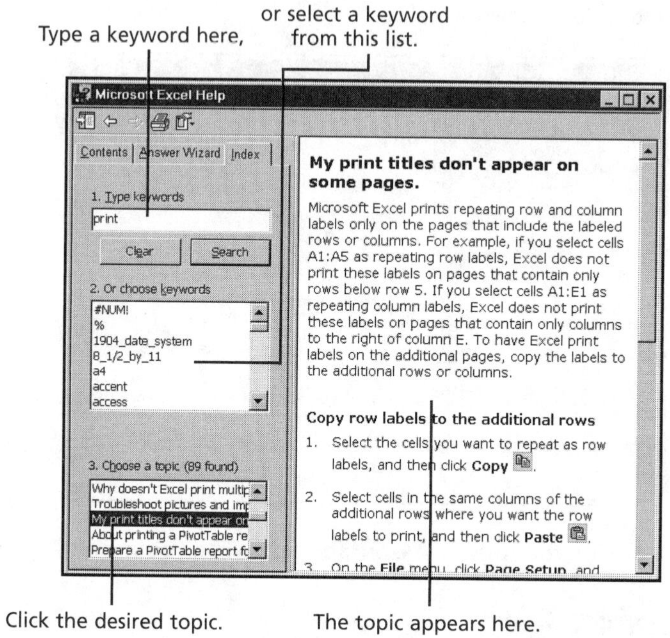

Type a keyword here,   or select a keyword
from this list.

Click the desired topic.   The topic appears here.

FIGURE 6.6   Browse through topics alphabetically with the Index.

In this lesson, you learned how to use the Office Assistant to get help, and how to find help on your own. In the next lesson, you'll learn how to get help online, get help with screen elements, and customize the Office Assistant.

LESSON 7
BEYOND HELP

In this lesson, you'll learn how to get help through the Internet, how to customize the Office Assistant, and how to get help with an onscreen element.

GOING ONLINE TO GET HELP

Although the Office Assistant is pretty helpful, sometimes it just can't help you locate the exact information you're looking for. If you have a connection to the Internet, you can go online and search Microsoft's own Web site for additional information. Follow these steps:

1. If you have not already done so, connect to the Internet in the usual manner.

2. If you can't find the topic you want after trying several times, select the topic None of the above, look for more help on the Web from those listed in the Office Assistant bubble.

3. A Help window appears, as shown in Figure 7.1. If you want to explain your question further, type additional information in the text box and click Send and go to the Web.

 Try, Try, Again If you'd like to give the Office Assistant another try, click Search tips in step 3, and you'll get some help in rephrasing your question.

4. Because you're sending information to the Internet, you'll probably see a security warning. Click Yes to continue.

5. You're connected to the Office Update Search site. Your question appears in the text box. Scroll down to the bottom of the screen,

and you'll see some links to pages within the site that may
answer your question. Click an answer to view that page.

6. If you don't find an answer that fits, try rewording the question
and clicking Search.

FIGURE 7.1   Ask Microsoft for help.

> Excel on the Web   Another way to get help is to visit
> the Excel Home page on the Microsoft Web site. Here
> you can browse frequently asked questions, download
> free add-on features, update your version of Excel,
> and more. To connect, establish your Internet connec-
> tion and then open the Help menu and select Office
> on the Web.

Turning the Office Assistant On or Off

Because the Office Assistant stays more or less out of the way, you can leave Office Assistant onscreen even when you're not using it. However, if you find the Office Assistant distracting, you can hide it temporarily:

> **Where's My Dialog Box?** If you leave the Office Assistant on and a warning dialog box (such as Would you like to save your changes?) needs to appear, it will show within the Office Assistant bubble. This doesn't affect how the dialog box works, but it is amusing, none the less.

- To hide the Office Assistant, right-click it and then select Hide.

- To make the Office Assistant reappear, click the Microsoft Excel Help button, or press F1.

> **Where Did It Go?** When you turn on the Office Assistant in Excel, it appears in your other Office programs as well. Likewise, if you turn off the Office Assistant while in Excel (whether temporarily or permanently), it also disappears from your other Office program windows.

If you prefer to get Help yourself (as explained in Lesson 6), you may want to turn the Office Assistant off permanently. Follow these steps:

1. Click the Options button in the Office Assistant bubble. The Office Assistant dialog box appears.

2. Select Use the Office Assistant to turn the option off, as shown in Figure 7.2.

3. Click OK.

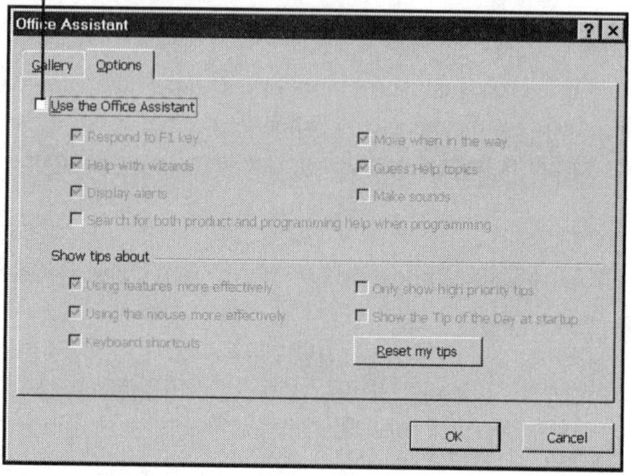

Deselect this option to turn the Office Assistant off forever!

FIGURE 7.2   You can turn off the Assistant permanently.

If you have a change of heart later, you can follow these same steps to turn the Use the Office Assistant option back on.

CHANGING TO A DIFFERENT OFFICE ASSISTANT

Clippit is not the only Office Assistant you can use. So if you find its antics annoying, follow these steps to change to a different assistant. (The help your assistant offers will remain the same—only the animations will be changed to protect the innocent.)

1. Click the Options button in the Office Assistant bubble. The Office Assistant dialog box appears.

2. Click the Gallery tab.

3. Click <Back or Next> to view other assistants, as shown in Figure 7.3.

4. When you find an assistant you like, click OK.

5. You may see a message telling you that this feature is not yet installed. If so, insert the CD-ROM containing Excel 2000, and click Yes.

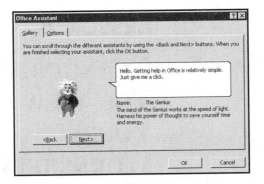

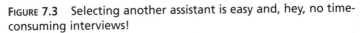

FIGURE 7.3   Selecting another assistant is easy and, hey, no time-consuming interviews!

GETTING HELP WITH SCREEN ELEMENTS

If you're wondering about the function of a particular button or tool on the screen, wonder no more. Just follow these steps to find out what it does:

1. Press Shift+F1, or open the Help menu and select What's This?. The mouse pointer changes to a question mark.

2. With the question mark pointer, click on the screen element for which you want help. A box appears explaining the element. Click anywhere in the worksheet to remove this box from the screen.

If you need help with an element in a dialog box, click the What's This? button at the right end of the title bar. (It looks like a big question mark.) Point to an element and click, and you'll get instant help.

In this lesson, you learned how to get help online, how to change the Office Assistant, and how to get help with an onscreen element. In the next lesson, you'll learn to change the way you view your Excel worksheet.

LESSON 8

CHANGING HOW YOU VIEW YOUR WORKSHEET

In this lesson, you will learn about the various ways in which you can view your worksheet.

There are many ways to change how your worksheet appears within the Excel window. Changing the view has no effect on how your worksheets will look when printed (unless you choose to hide data onscreen), but changing the view and getting a different perspective helps you see your data more clearly. For example, you can enlarge or reduce the size of the text to view more or less of the worksheet at one time. You also can "freeze" row or column labels so you won't lose your place as you scroll through a large worksheet.

MAGNIFYING AND REDUCING THE WORKSHEET VIEW

To enlarge or reduce your view of the current worksheet, use the Zoom feature. Click the Zoom button on the Standard toolbar and select the zoom percentage you want to use, such as 25% or 200%. If you want to zoom by a number that's not listed, type the amount in the Zoom box and press Enter. In addition, you can enlarge a specific area of the worksheet by selecting it first, opening the Zoom menu, and choosing Selection.

> **Fast Zoom** If you use the Microsoft IntelliMouse, you can zoom in and out quickly by pressing and holding the Ctrl key as you move the wheel forward or back.

You also can display your worksheet so that it takes up the full screen—eliminating toolbars, Formula bar, status bar, and so on—as shown in Figure 8.1. To do so, open the View menu and select Full Screen. To return to Normal view, click Close Full Screen.

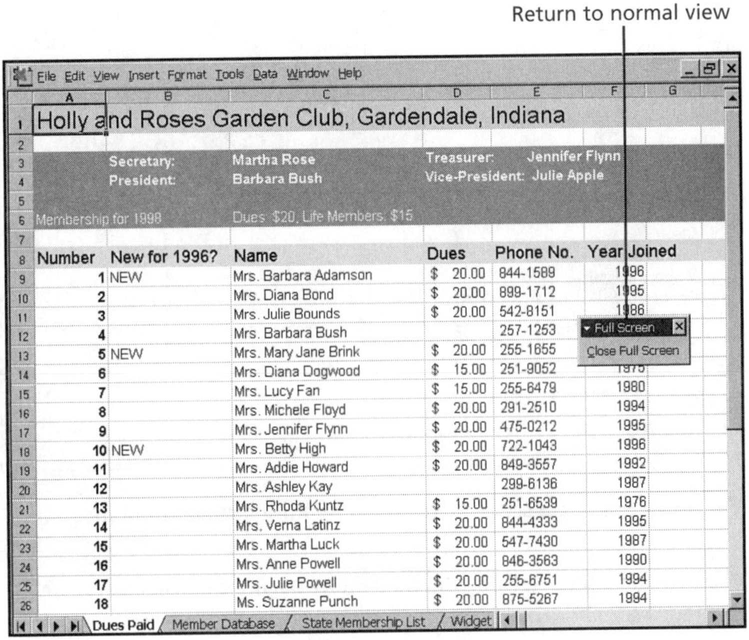

Return to normal view

FIGURE 8.1 View your worksheet in a full window.

FREEZING COLUMN AND ROW LABELS

As you scroll through a large worksheet, it's often helpful to freeze your column and row labels so that you can view them with related data. For example, as you can see in Figure 8.2, it's helpful to view the column and row headings to understand the data in the cells.

To freeze row or column headings (or both), follow these steps:

1. Click the cell to the *right* of the row labels and/or *below* any column labels you want to freeze. This highlights the cell.

2. Open the Window menu and select Freeze Panes.

Frozen row labels   Frozen column labels

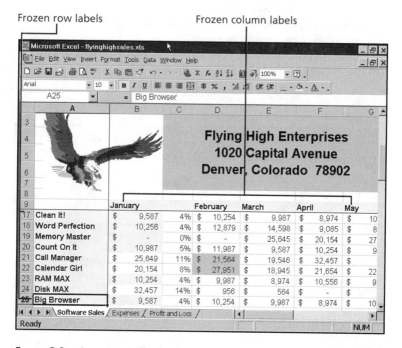

FIGURE 8.2   As you scroll, the frozen headings remain in place.

Play around a little, moving the cursor all around the document. As you do, the row and/or column headings remain locked in their positions. This enables you to view data in other parts of the worksheet without losing track of what that data represents. To unlock headings, open the Window menu again and select Unfreeze Panes.

SPLITTING WORKSHEETS

Sometimes when you're working with a large worksheet, you find yourself wanting to view two parts of it at one time to compare data, or to copy or move it. To view two parts of a worksheet, you *split* it. Figure 8.3 shows a split worksheet.

Follow these steps to split a worksheet:

1. Click and hold either the vertical or the horizontal split box.

2. Drag the split bar into the worksheet window.

3. Drop the split bar to divide the window at that location. When you scroll, the two panes automatically scroll in synch. For example, if you split the worksheet horizontally and then scroll right or left, the two panes are in synch.

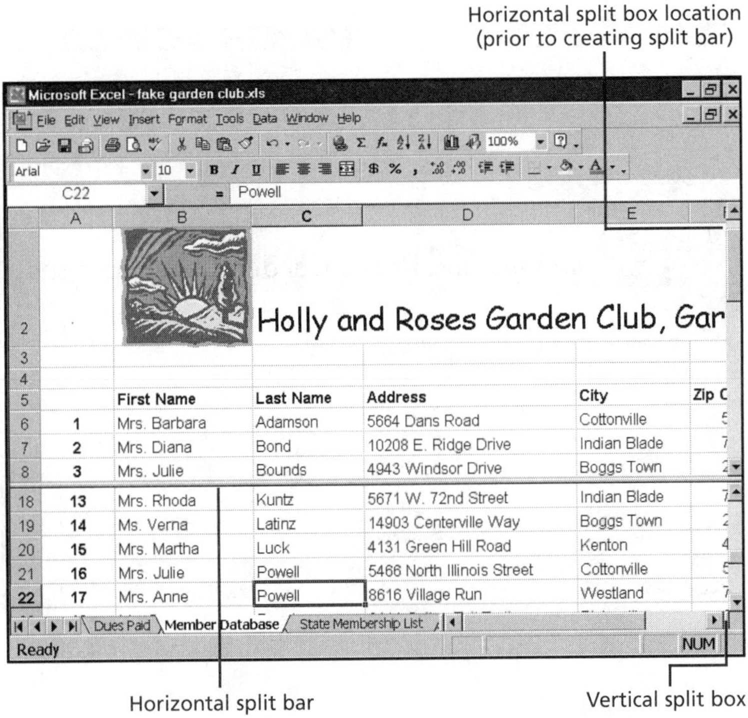

Horizontal split box location
(prior to creating split bar)

Horizontal split bar   Vertical split box

FIGURE 8.3   Split a worksheet to view two parts at one time.

To remove the split, drag it back to its original position on the scrollbar, or double-click the split bar.

HIDING WORKBOOKS, WORKSHEETS, COLUMNS, AND ROWS

For those times when you're working on top-secret information, you can hide workbooks, worksheets, columns or rows from prying eyes. For example, if you have confidential data stored in one particular worksheet, you can hide that worksheet, yet still be able to view the other worksheets in that workbook. You can also hide particular columns (see Figure 8.4) or rows within a worksheet—even an entire workbook if you want.

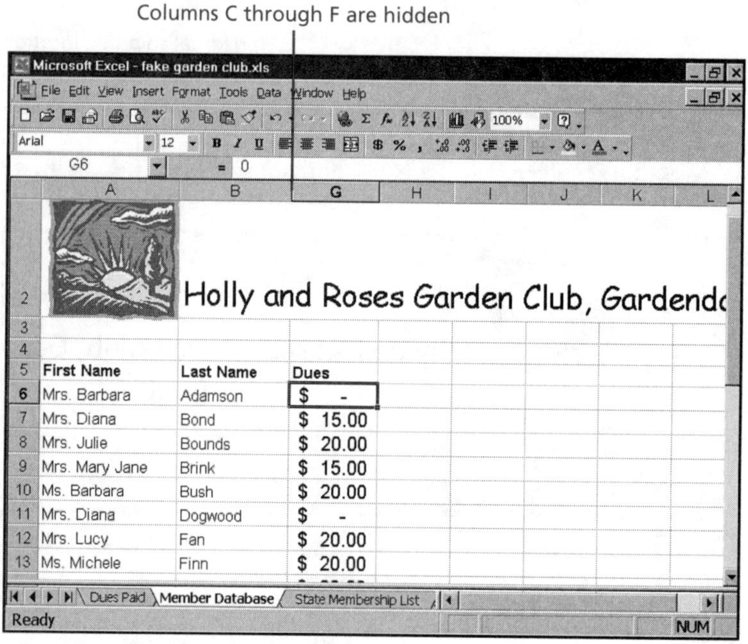

Columns C through F are hidden

FIGURE 8.4   Hide data to prevent it from being viewed, printed, or changed.

In addition to hiding data to prevent it from appearing on a report, you might hide it to prevent it from accidentally being changed. When data is hidden, it cannot be viewed, printed, or changed. (This is unlike the other changes you've learned about in this chapter, which just modify the worksheet view, such as zooming the worksheet.)

Use these methods to hide data:

- To hide a row or a column in a worksheet, click a row or column heading to select it. Then right-click within the row or column, and select Hide from the shortcut menu that appears.

- To hide a worksheet, click its tab to select it. Then open the Format menu, select Sheet, and select Hide.

- To hide an entire workbook, open the Window menu and select Hide.

 Hide More Than One   To select several worksheets, press and hold Ctrl while you click each tab. To select several rows or columns, press and hold Ctrl while you click each heading.

Of course, whenever you need to, you can easily redisplay the hidden data. To redisplay hidden data, select the hidden area first. For example, select the rows, columns, or sheets adjacent to the hidden ones. Then repeat the previous steps, selecting Unhide from the appropriate menu.

You Can't Hide It Completely!   It's easy to undo the command to hide data, so you can't really hide data completely as a means of security. If you give the workbook file to someone else, for example, he or she could unhide and view the data you have hidden.

In this lesson, you learned how to change the view of your worksheet, freeze column and row headings, and hide data. In the next lesson, you will learn how to enter data into an Excel worksheet.

LESSON 9

ENTERING DIFFERENT TYPES OF DATA

In this lesson, you will learn how to enter different types of data in an Excel worksheet.

There are many types of data that you can enter into your worksheets, including text, numbers, dates, times, formulas, and functions. In this lesson, you'll learn how to enter text, numbers, dates, and times. In Lessons 18, 19, and 20 you'll learn how to enter formulas and functions.

ENTERING TEXT

Text is any combination of letters, numbers, and spaces. By default, text is automatically left-aligned in a cell.

To enter text into a cell:

1. Select the cell in which you want to enter text.

2. Type the text. As you type, your text appears in the cell and in the Formula bar, as shown in Figure 9.1.

3. Press Enter. Your text appears in the cell, left-aligned. (You can also press Tab or an arrow key to enter the text *and* move to another cell.) If you've made a mistake and you want to abandon your entry, press Esc instead.

But It Doesn't Fit!   When text does not fit into a cell, it "overflows" into the next cell, provided that cell is empty. If it is not, then the text is cut off. To expand a cell to display the data, you widen the column it's in: move the mouse pointer to the right-hand edge of the column's heading, then double-click. See Lesson 14 for more help.

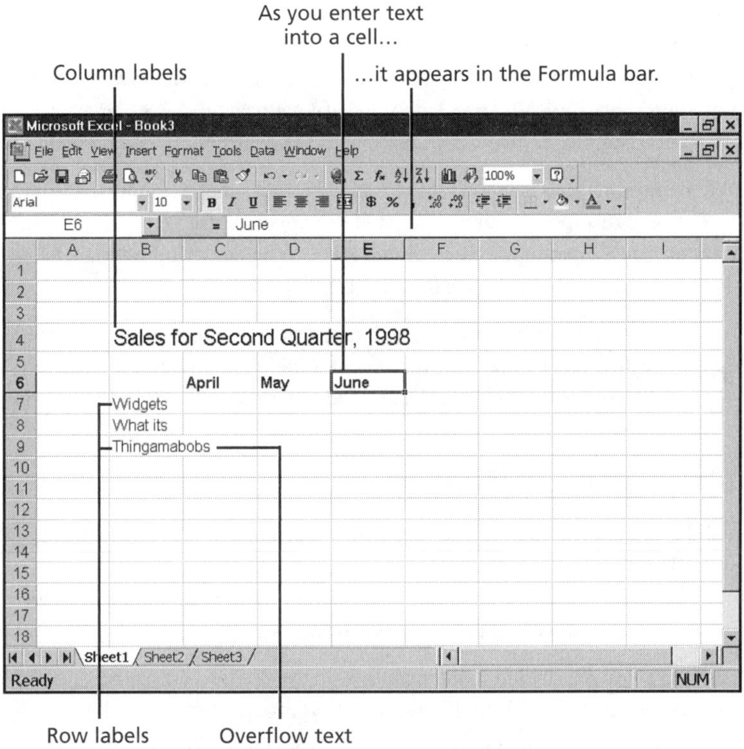

As you enter text
into a cell...

Column labels   ...it appears in the Formula bar.

FIGURE 9.1 Data that you enter also appears in the Formula bar as
you type it.

> **Entering Numbers As Text** To enter a number that
> will be treated as text (such as a zip code), precede
> the entry with a single quotation mark, as in '46220.
> The single quotation mark is an alignment prefix that
> tells Excel to treat the following characters as text and
> left-align them in the cell.

TIPS ON ENTERING COLUMN AND ROW LABELS

Column and row labels identify your data. Column labels appear across
the top of the worksheet beneath the worksheet title (if any). Row labels
are entered on the left side of the worksheet.

Column labels describe what the numbers in a column represent. Typically, column labels specify time intervals such as years, months, days, quarters, and so on. Row labels describe what the numbers in each row represent. Typically, row labels specify data categories, such as product names, employee names, or income and expense items in a budget.

When entering your column labels, enter the first label, then press the Tab key instead of pressing Enter. This will move you to the next cell on the right so you can enter another column label. When entering row labels, use the down arrow key instead of the Tab key.

If you need to enter similar data (such as a series of months or years) as column or row labels, there's a way to enter them quickly. See the section, "Entering a Series of Numbers, Dates, and Other Data," later in this lesson.

ENTERING NUMBERS

Valid numbers can include the numeric characters 0–9 and any of these special characters: + – / . , $ %. This means that you can include commas, decimal points, dollar signs, percent signs, and parentheses with the numbers that you enter into your worksheet.

Although you can include punctuation when you type your entries, you may not want to. For example, instead of typing a column of dollar amounts complete with dollar signs, commas, and decimal points, you could type just the numbers, such as 700 and 81295, and then *format* the column with currency formatting. Excel would then change your entries to $700.00 and $81,295.00 or to $700 and $81295, depending on the number of decimal points you specify. By not entering the dollar signs, commas, and decimal points yourself, you save time and give yourself the ability to change the format later on if you like. See Lesson 21 for more information on how to format numbers.

To enter a number:

1. Select the cell into which you want to enter a number.

2. Type the number. To enter a negative number, precede it with a minus sign or surround it with parentheses. To enter a fraction, precede it with a 0, as in 0 1/2. Note that you must type a space between the 0 and the fraction.

3. Press Enter, and the number appears in the cell, right-aligned.

Pound Signs Giving You a Pounding Headache? If you enter a number and it appears in the cell as all pound signs (######) or in scientific notation (such as 7.78E+06), don't worry—the number is okay. The cell just isn't wide enough to display the entire number. To fix it, double-click on the right border of the column's heading. The column expands to fit the largest entry. See Lesson 14 for more help on changing column widths.

ENTERING DATES AND TIMES

After you enter a date or time into a cell, Excel converts the date into a number that reflects the number of days between January 1, 1900 and that date. Even though you won't see this number (Excel displays your entry as a normal date), the number is used whenever you use this date in a calculation.

Follow these steps to enter a date or time:

1. Select the cell into which you want to enter a date or time.

2. To enter a date, use the format, MM/DD/YY, or the format, MM-DD-YY, as in 5/9/98 or 5-9-98.

    To enter a time, be sure to specify AM or PM, as in 7:21 p, or 8:22 a.

 Day or Night? Unless you type AM or PM after your time entry, Excel assumes that you are using a 24-hour military clock. Therefore, 8:20 is assumed to be AM, not PM. So if you mean PM, type the entry as 8:20 PM (or 8:20 p). Note that you must type a space between the time and the AM or PM notation.

3. Press Enter. As long as Excel recognizes the entry as a date or time, it appears right-aligned in the cell. If Excel doesn't recognize it, it's treated as text and left-aligned.

Now, after you enter your date or time, you can format the cells to display the date or time exactly as you want it to appear, as September 16, 1998, and 16:50 (military time), for example. If you're entering a column of dates or times, you can format the entire column in one easy step. If you like, you can specify the format you want before you enter any data. Then, when you type your dates or times, Excel will automatically change them to fit that format. To format a column, click the column header to select the column. Then open the Format menu and select Cells. On the Numbers tab, select the date or time format you want. (See Lesson 21 for more information.)

If you enter a long date and it appears in the cell as all number signs (#######), Excel is trying to tell you that the column is not wide enough to display it. To widen the column, double-click the right-hand border of the column's header.

Copying (Filling) the Same Data to Other Cells

You can copy (fill) an entry into surrounding cells by performing the following steps:

1. Click the fill handle of the cell whose contents you want to copy.

2. Drag the fill handle down or to the right to copy the data to adjacent cells (see Figure 9.2). A bubble appears to let you know exactly what data is being copied.

 Watch That Fill!   Existing data (if any) in the adjacent cells to which you fill will be replaced by the data you're copying. If you accidentally replace data you meant to keep, click Undo.

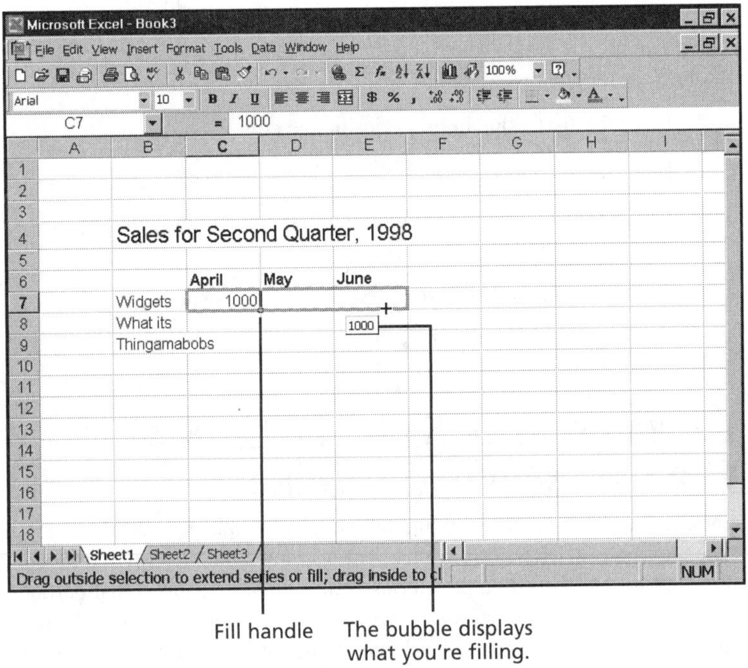

Fill handle   The bubble displays
what you're filling.

FIGURE 9.2   Drag the fill handle to copy the contents and formatting into neighboring cells.

ENTERING A SERIES OF NUMBERS, DATES, AND OTHER DATA

Entering a *series* (such as January, February, and March or 1998, 1999, and 2000) is similar to filling a cell's contents. As you drag the fill handle of the original cell, Excel analyzes the first entry and creates a series of entries based on it. For example, if you type Monday in a cell, and then drag the cell's fill handle over some adjacent cells, you'll create the series Monday, Tuesday, Wednesday.... As you drag, the bubble lets you know exactly what you're filling so that you can stop at the appropriate cell to create exactly the series you want.

If you're filling a number, a month, or other item that might be interpreted as a series (such as January, February, and so on), and you don't want to create a series—you just want to copy the contents of the cell exactly—then press and hold the Ctrl key as you drag the fill handle.

If you want to create a series such as 10, 20, 30, and so on, and Excel doesn't create the series when you drag the fill handle, or it creates the wrong series, here's what to do:

1. Enter the first value in the series in one cell.

2. Enter the second value in the series in the next cell.

3. Select both cells by clicking on the first cell and dragging over the second cell.

4. Drag the fill handle as usual. Excel will analyze the two cells, see the pattern, and recreate it.

ENTERING THE SAME DATA IN A COLUMN OVER AND OVER

Entering the same values over and over in a column is easy. When you type the first few letters of an entry, AutoComplete intelligently completes the entry for you based on the entries you've already made in that particular column. (AutoComplete works with data entered in columns only, not rows.) For example, suppose you want to enter the countries of origin for a series of packages. You type the name of a country once, and the next time you start to type that entry, AutoComplete inserts it for you.

By default, AutoComplete is always turned on, so you don't have to worry about that. Follow these steps to try out AutoComplete:

1. Type **England** into a cell and press the down arrow key to move to the next cell down. Type **Spain** and press the down arrow key again. Then type **Italy** and press the down arrow key.

2. Type **e**, and "England" appears in the cell. Press Enter to accept the entry. (Likewise, if you type **i** or **s**, "Italy" or "Spain" will appear.)

3. If you'd like to try an alternate method of using AutoComplete, right-click a cell and select Pick From List from the shortcut menu. Excel shows you a PickList of entries (in alphabetical order) that it has automatically created from the words you've typed in the column.

4. Click a word in the PickList to insert it in the selected cell.

In this lesson, you learned how to enter different types of data and how to automate data entry. In the next lesson, you will learn how to edit entries.

LESSON 10
CORRECTING YOUR ENTRIES

In this lesson, you will learn how to change data and how to undo those changes if necessary. You'll also learn how to search for data and replace it with other data, and to spell check your work.

MAKING CHANGES TO DATA

After you have entered data into a cell, you can make changes to it in either the Formula bar or in the cell itself.

To make changes to a cell:

1. Select the cell in which you want to edit data.

2. To begin editing, click in the Formula bar. If you want to edit within the cell itself, press F2 or double-click the cell. This puts you in Edit mode; the word Edit appears in the status bar.

3. Press ← or → to move the insertion point within the entry. Press the Backspace key to delete characters to the left of the insertion point; press the Delete key to delete characters to the right. Then type any characters you want to add.

4. Click the Enter button on the Formula bar or press Enter on the keyboard to accept your changes.

   Or, if you change your mind and you no longer want to edit your entry, click the Cancel button or press Esc.

UNDOING AN ACTION

You can undo just about anything you do while working in Excel, including any changes you make to a cell's data. To undo a change, click the

Undo button on the Standard toolbar.

To undo an Undo (reinstate a change), click the Redo button in the Standard toolbar.

> **Undoing/Redoing More Than One Thing**   When you click the Undo or Redo button, Excel undoes or repeats only the most recent action. To undo (or redo) some previous action, click the drop-down arrow on the button and select the action you want from the list. You also can click the Undo button multiple times to undo a series of previous actions one at a time.

FINDING AND REPLACING DATA

With Excel's Find and Replace features, you can locate data in the worksheet and replace it with new data. So if you have a label, value, or formula that is entered incorrectly throughout the worksheet, you can use the Edit, Replace command to find and replace all occurrences of the incorrect information with the correct data.

To find and replace data, follow these steps:

1. Open the **Edit** menu and select **Replace**. The Replace dialog box appears, as shown in Figure 10.1.

Type the data you want to find.   Find the next occurrence.

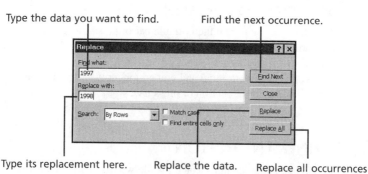

Type its replacement here.   Replace the data.   Replace all occurrences of the data.

FIGURE 10.1   Find and replace data with the Replace dialog box.

2. Type the text you want to find in the Find what text box.

3. Click in the Replace with text box and type the text you want to use as replacement text.

4. In the Search box, indicate whether you want to search for your entry by rows or by columns.

5. If you want to match the exact case of your entry, click the Match case check box. If you want to locate cells that contain exactly what you entered (and no additional data), click the Find entire cells only check box.

6. Click Find Next to find the first occurrence of your specified text.

7. When an occurrence is found, it is highlighted. Click Replace to replace only this occurrence or Replace All to replace all occurrences of the data you specified in the worksheet.

Even if you don't need to correct an entry, you can use the Find feature to locate a specific entry in your worksheet so you can view it. Select Edit, Find, then type the data you want to locate in the Find what text box and click Find Next.

CHECKING YOUR SPELLING

Excel offers a spell-checking feature that rapidly finds and corrects misspellings in a worksheet.

To run the spelling checker, follow these steps:

1. Click the Spelling button on the Standard toolbar. Excel finds the first misspelled word and displays it at the top of the Spelling dialog box. A suggested correction then appears in the Change to box (see Figure 10.2).

2. To accept the suggestion in the Change to box, click Change. Or, click Change All to change all occurrences of the misspelled word.

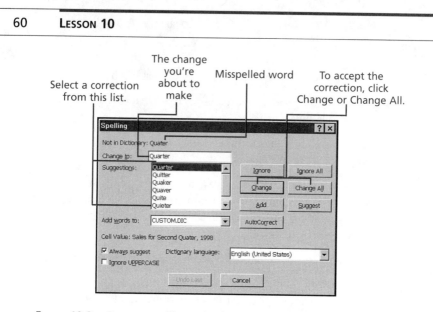

FIGURE **10.2** Correct spelling mistakes with the options in the Spelling dialog box.

3. If the suggestion in the Change to box is not correct, you can do any of the following:

- Select a different suggestion from the Suggestions box, and then click Change or Change All. (You can display additional words in the Suggestions list by clicking Suggest.)

- Type your own correction in the Change to box, and then click Change or Change All.

- Click Ignore to leave the word unchanged.

- Click Ignore All to leave all occurrences of the word unchanged.

- Click Add to add the word to the dictionary so Excel won't flag it as misspelled again.

- Click AutoCorrect to add a correctly spelled word to the AutoCorrect list, so that Excel can correct it automatically as you type.

4. You may see a message asking you if you want to continue checking spelling at the beginning of the sheet. If so, click Yes to continue. When the spelling checker can't find any more misspelled words, it displays a prompt telling you that the spelling check is complete. Click OK to confirm that the spelling check is finished.

Correct Something Incorrectly? If you mistakenly select the wrong option, you can click the Undo Last button in the Spelling dialog box to undo the last change you made.

In this lesson, you learned how to edit cell data and undo changes. In addition, you learned how to spell check your worksheet. In the next lesson, you will learn how to select and name ranges of data.

LESSON 11

WORKING WITH RANGES

In this lesson, you will learn how to select and name ranges.

WHAT IS A RANGE?

A *range* is a rectangular group of connected cells. The cells in a range
may all be in one column, or one row, or any combination of columns and
rows, as long as the range forms a rectangle, as shown in Figure 11.1. A
range also can be a single cell.

Ranges are referred to by their *anchor points* (the upper-left corner and
the lower-right corner). For example, the ranges shown in Figure 11.1
include C10:I14, B16:I16, and H20.

Learning how to use ranges can save you time. For example, you can
select a range and use it to format a group of cells with one step. You can
use a range to print only a selected group of cells. You can also use ranges
in formulas.

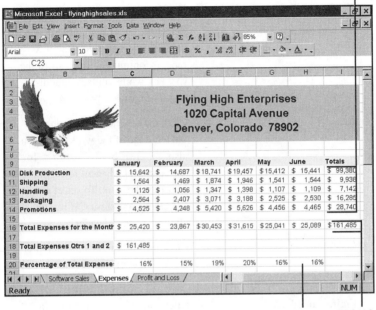

C10:I14

H20   B16:I16

FIGURE 11.1   A range is any combination of cells that forms a rectangle.

SELECTING A RANGE

To select a range using the mouse, follow these steps:

1. Move the mouse pointer to the upper-left corner of a range.

2. Click and hold the left mouse button.

3. Drag the mouse to the lower-right corner of the range and release the mouse button. The selected range is highlighted.

Techniques that you can use to quickly select a row, a column, an entire worksheet, or several ranges, are shown in Table 11.1.

TABLE 11.1   SELECTION TECHNIQUES

TO SELECT THIS...	DO THIS...
Several ranges	Select the first range, hold down the Ctrl key, and select the next range. Continue holding down the Ctrl key while you select additional ranges.
Row	Click the row heading number at the left edge of the worksheet. You also can press Shift+Spacebar. To select several adjacent rows, drag over their headers. To select non-adjacent rows, press Ctrl as you click each row's header.
Column	Click the column heading letter at the top edge of the worksheet. You also can press Ctrl+Spacebar.
Entire worksheet	Click the Select All button (the blank rectangle in the upper-left corner of the work-sheet, above row 1 and left of column A). You also can press Ctrl+A.
The same range on several worksheets	Press and hold Ctrl as you click the worksheets you want to use, then select the range in the usual way.
Range that is out of view	Press Ctrl+G (Go To) or click in the Name box on the Formula bar, and type the address of the range you want to select. For example, to select the range R100 to T250, type **R100:T250** and press Enter.

Deselecting a Selection   If you decide not to select a range, you can remove the range selection by clicking any cell in the worksheet.

 A New Look!   When you select cells now, you'll notice that they are not highlighted in reverse video, but in a slightly grayed tone, so you can still read your data.

NAMING RANGES

Up to this point, you have used cell addresses to refer to single cells and ranges. Although that works, it is often more convenient to name important cells with more recognizable names. For example, say you want to determine your net income by subtracting expenses from income (see Lesson 18). You can name the cell that contains your total income: "INCOME," and name the cell that contains your total expenses: "EXPENSES." You can then determine your net income by using the formula:

```
=INCOME-EXPENSES
```

Giving important cells memorable names will make adding formulas to your worksheet more logical and easier to manage. You can also use a range name or cell name to jump to a specific part of the worksheet by typing the name in the Name box on the Formula bar (or selecting it from the Name list), as explained in Lesson 5. This technique not only displays the range you want, but selects it too! In addition, you can use named cell ranges to help you create charts, as explained in Lesson 24.

You don't necessarily need to name all your ranges in order to use them in formulas. You can use your column and row labels instead. See Lesson 18 for details.

Follow these steps to name a range:

1. Select the range you want to name (the cells must be located on the same worksheet). If you want to name a single cell, then simply click it.

2. Click in the Name box on the left side of the Formula bar (see Figure 11.2).

Type the range name here.   Selected area

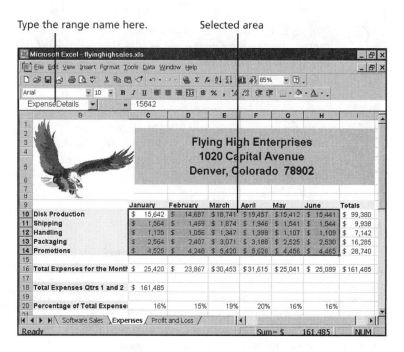

FIGURE 11.2   Creating a name for a selected range.

3. Type a range name using up to 255 characters. Valid names can include letters, numbers, periods, and underlines, *but no spaces.* In addition, a number cannot be used as the first character in the range name, and a range name cannot look like a cell address such as B14.

4. Press Enter.

To see your list of range names, click the Name box's drop-down arrow (on the Formula bar). To quickly select a named range, open the Name list and choose the range you want.

Another way to name a range is to select it, open the Insert menu, select Name, and choose Define. This displays the Define Name dialog box shown in Figure 11.3. Type a name in the Names in workbook text box and click OK.

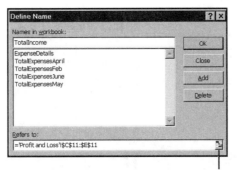

Collapse Dialog button

FIGURE **11.3**   The Define Name dialog box.

The Define Name dialog box enables you to see the range to which a range name refers, and to adjust that range if needed. Click a range name in the Names in workbook list, and you'll see the cell address currently assigned to the range name in the Refers to text box. To adjust the range to which the name refers, type a new range or click the Collapse Dialog button and select a range in the worksheet.

This dialog box also lets you delete range names. Just click a name in the Names in workbook list and click the Delete button.

> **Constant Value or Formula**   You can use the Define Name dialog box to assign a name to a constant value, such as 120%, or a formula. Just type a name in the Names in workbook text box, then type the value or formula in the Refers to text box and click OK.

In this lesson, you learned how to select and name ranges. In the next lesson, you will learn how to copy, move, and delete ranges of cells.

LESSON 12

COPYING, MOVING, AND DELETING RANGES

In this lesson, you will learn how to copy, move, and delete large groups of cells (ranges).

COPYING DATA

In Lesson 9, you learned how to speed up data entry by copying the same data to adjacent cells using the fill handle. In this lesson, you'll learn how to copy data anywhere in the worksheet, or to other worksheets or workbooks.

When you copy or move data, a copy of that data is placed in a temporary storage area called the Clipboard. This Clipboard enables you to copy data anywhere, even into documents created by other programs. When you copy, the original data remains in its place and a copy of it is placed where you indicate.

> **What Is the Clipboard?** The *Clipboard* is an area of memory that is accessible to all Windows programs. The Clipboard is used to copy or move data from place to place within a program or between programs. The techniques that you learn here are the same ones used in all Windows programs.

Follow these steps to copy data:

1. Select the cell that you want to copy. You can select any range or several ranges if you want. (See Lesson 11.)

2. Click the Copy button on the Standard toolbar. The contents of the selected cell are copied to the Clipboard.

3. Select the first cell in the area where you would like to place the copy. (To copy the data to another worksheet or workbook, change to that worksheet or workbook first.)

4. Click the Paste button. Excel inserts the contents of the Clipboard at the location of the insertion point.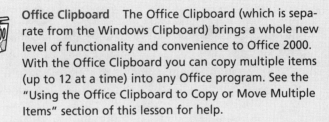

Office Clipboard   The Office Clipboard (which is separate from the Windows Clipboard) brings a whole new level of functionality and convenience to Office 2000. With the Office Clipboard you can copy multiple items (up to 12 at a time) into any Office program. See the "Using the Office Clipboard to Copy or Move Multiple Items" section of this lesson for help.

Watch Out!   When copying or moving data, be careful not to paste the data over existing data (unless, of course, you intend to).

You can copy the same data to several places by repeating the Paste command. Data copied to the Clipboard remains there until you copy or cut (move) something else (unless you clear the Office Clipboard, which also clears the Windows Clipboard—see the "Using the Office Clipboard to Copy or Move Multiple Items" section in this lesson.

Don't Forget the Shortcut Menu   When cutting, copying, and pasting data, don't forget the shortcut menu. Select the cells you want to cut or copy, right-click, and choose the appropriate command from the shortcut menu that appears.

USING DRAG AND DROP TO COPY DATA

The fastest way to copy something is to drag and drop it. Select the cells you want to copy, hold down the Ctrl key, and drag the border of the range you selected (see Figure 12.1). When you release the mouse button, the contents are copied to the new location. (If you forget to hold down the Ctrl key, Excel moves the data instead of copying it.) To insert the data between existing cells, press Ctrl+Shift as you drag.

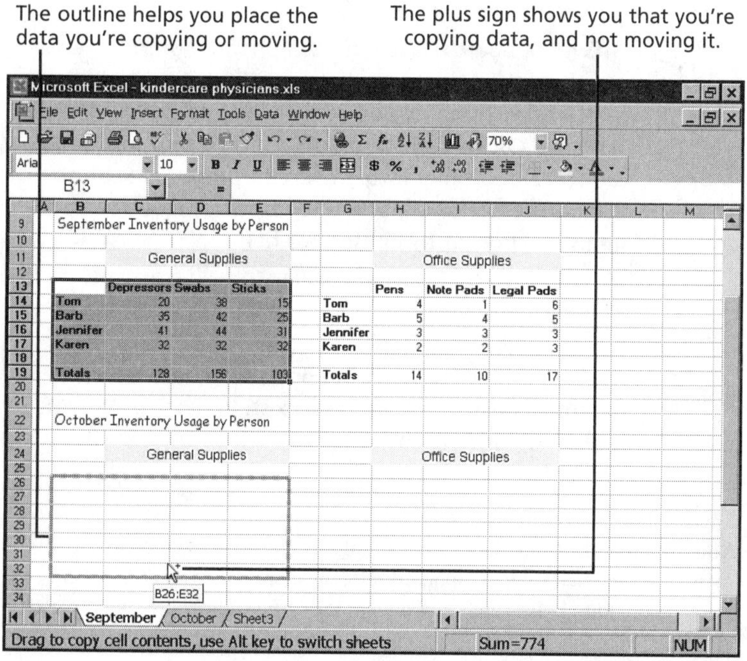

The outline helps you place the data you're copying or moving.

The plus sign shows you that you're copying data, and not moving it.

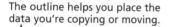

FIGURE 12.1   Dragging is the fastest way to copy or move data.

To drag a copy to a different sheet, press Ctrl+Alt as you drag the selection to the sheet's tab. Excel switches you to that sheet, where you can drop your selection in the appropriate location.

MOVING DATA

Moving data is similar to copying except that the data is removed from its original place and placed in the new location.

To move data, follow these steps:

1. Select the cells you want to move.

2. Click the Cut button.

3. Select the first cell in the area where you would like to place the data. To move the data to another worksheet, change to that worksheet.

4. Click Paste.

USING DRAG AND DROP TO MOVE DATA

To move data quickly, use the drag and drop feature. Select the data to be moved, and then drag the border of the selected cells to its new location. To insert the data between existing cells, press Shift while you drag. To move the data to a different worksheet, press the Alt key and drag the selection to the worksheet's tab. You're then switched to that sheet, where you can drop your selection at the appropriate point.

USING THE OFFICE CLIPBOARD TO COPY OR MOVE MULTIPLE ITEMS

The Office Clipboard allows you to copy or move multiple bits of data (as many as 12 separate items) to any of your other Office programs. For example, you could copy several parts of your Excel worksheet (maybe data stored on separate worksheets), a graphic, and even a chart from a PowerPoint slide, and then paste them all into a Word document. Actually, you can copy data from any document, but you can only paste the multiple items into an Office document. If you try to paste data into a non-Office document, you'll paste only the last item you copied (which is the same as if you were using only the Windows Clipboard).

 What a Drag! You can't use the drag and drop feature to copy or move data to the Office Clipboard.

To use the Office Clipboard:

1. Display the Clipboard toolbar (see Figure 12.2) by opening the View menu, selecting Toolbars, then selecting Clipboard.

Click here to paste all the items.

To clear the Clipboard, click here.

To paste just this item, click it.

FIGURE 12.2   The new Office Clipboard toolbar.

2. Select the item you want to copy or move, then click the Copy button or the Cut button on the Standard toolbar of any Office program (and most other programs as well), or just use the Edit, Copy and Edit, Cut commands in any program.

> **What About the Windows Clipboard?**   When you're copying items to the Office Clipboard, the last item you copy or move is also placed on the Windows Clipboard. So if you try to paste something to a non-Office program, the last item is all that will be pasted.

3. After you're done collecting the items you want to copy or move, switch to any Office program, and click the Paste All button on the Clipboard toolbar.

To paste only a single item from the Office Clipboard, just click that item. (To clear the Office Clipboard and start over, click the Clear Clipboard button. This clears the Windows Clipboard as well.)

There are a few things to keep in mind when using the Office Clipboard to paste multiple items. One, if you select a cell that contains a formula, and you paste it into another program's document, such as Word, you will not paste the formula itself, but the result of the formula (the value currently shown in the cell). Two, if you select multiple ranges in Excel and then paste them, they'll be pasted along one column. And three, if you've copied a drawing or clip art picture to the Office Clipboard, you will not be able to use the Paste All button while in Excel. (You can still paste an individual item by clicking it.)

DELETING DATA

To delete the data in a cell or range of cells, select it and press Delete. However, Excel offers additional options for deleting cells:

- With the Edit, Clear command, you can delete just the formatting of a cell (or an attached comment), without deleting its contents. The formatting of a cell includes the cell's color, border style, numeric format, font size, and so on. You'll learn more about this option in a moment.

- With the Edit, Delete command, you can remove cells and then shift surrounding cells over to take their place. This option is covered in Lesson 13.

To use the Clear command to remove the formatting of a cell or a note, follow these steps:

1. Select the cells you want to clear.

2. Open the Edit menu and select Clear. The Clear submenu appears.

3. Select the desired clear option: All (which clears the cells of all contents, formatting, and notes), Formats, Contents, or Comments.

In this lesson, you learned how to copy, move, and delete data. In the next lesson, you will learn how to insert columns and rows into your worksheet, and to remove them when needed.

LESSON 13

INSERTING AND REMOVING CELLS, ROWS, AND COLUMNS

In this lesson, you will learn how to rearrange the data in your worksheet by adding and removing cells, rows, and columns.

INSERTING ROWS AND COLUMNS

Inserting entire rows and columns in your worksheet is easy. Here's what you do:

1. To insert a single row or column, select the cell to the *right* of where you want to insert a column, or *below* where you want to insert a row.

    To insert multiple columns or rows, select the number of columns or rows you want to insert. To insert columns, drag over the column letters at the top of the worksheet. To insert rows, drag over the row numbers. For example, select three column letters or row numbers to insert three rows or columns.

2. Open the Insert menu and select Rows or Columns. Excel inserts row above your selection; column to the left of your selection. The inserted rows or columns contain the same formatting as the cells you selected in step 1. Figure 13.1 simulates a worksheet before and after two rows were inserted.

> **Fast Insert** To quickly insert rows or columns, select one or more rows or columns, right-click one of them, and choose Insert from the shortcut menu.

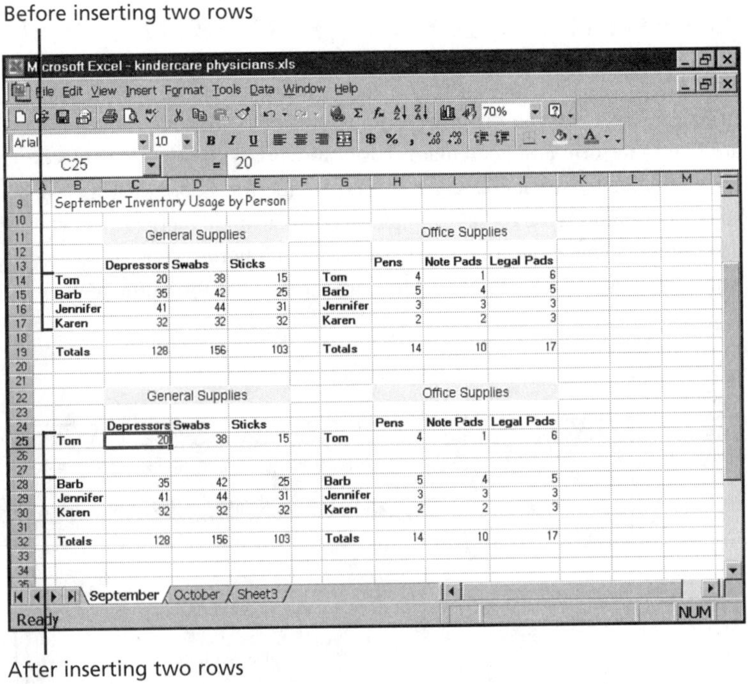

Before inserting two rows

After inserting two rows

FIGURE **13.1** Inserting two rows in a worksheet.

REMOVING ROWS AND COLUMNS

When you delete a row in your worksheet, the rows below the deleted row move *up* to fill the space. When you delete a column, the columns to the right shift *left*.

Follow these steps to delete a row or column:

1. Click the row number or column letter of the row or column you want to delete. You can select more than one row or column by dragging over the row numbers or column letters.

2. Open the Edit menu and choose Delete. Excel deletes the row or column and renumbers the remaining rows and columns sequentially. All cell references in formulas are updated appropriately, unless they are absolute values (see Lesson 18 for more information on absolute values).

MERGING CELLS TOGETHER TO FORM ONE LARGE CELL

In Excel 2000, you can merge the data in one cell with adjacent cells (that are blank) to form a big cell that is easier to work with. Merging cells is especially handy when creating a decorative title for the top of your worksheet (see Figure 13.2 for an example). Within a single merged cell, you can quickly change the font, point size, color and border style of your title. (See Lessons 21, 22, and 23 to learn more about formatting cells.)

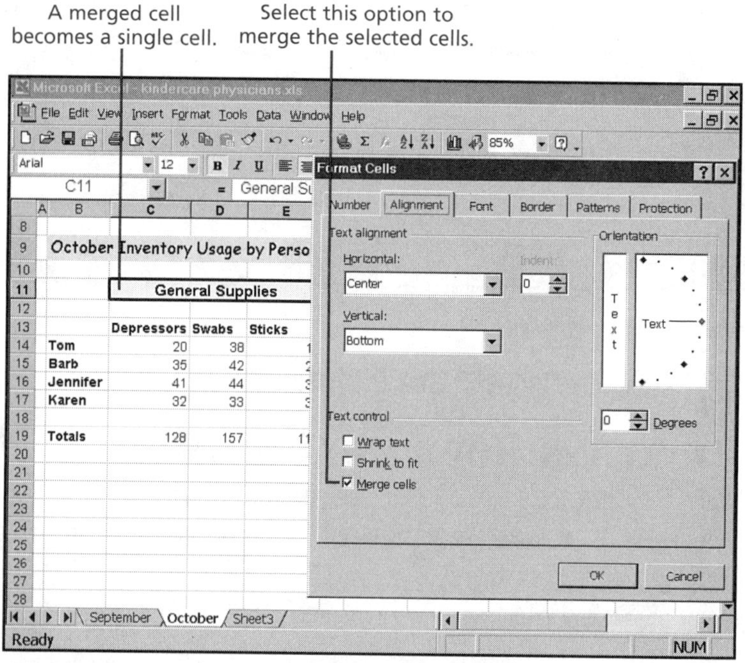

A merged cell becomes a single cell.   Select this option to merge the selected cells.

FIGURE 13.2   Merge cells to form a single cell.

To create a title with merged cells, follow these steps:

1. Type your title in the upper-left cell of the range you want to use for your heading. If you have a multi-line title, press Alt+Enter to insert each new line.

2. Select the range in which you want to place your title.

3. Open the Format menu and select Cells. The Format Cells dialog box appears.

4. Click the Alignment tab.

5. Click the Merge cells check box. You may also want to make adjustments to the text within the merged cells. For example, you may want to select Center in the Vertical drop-down list to center the text vertically within the cell.

6. Click OK when you're done. The selected cells are merged into a single cell, which you can format as needed.

You can quickly merge selected cells and center the data in the left-most cell by clicking the Merge and Center button on the Formatting toolbar.

INSERTING CELLS BETWEEN EXISTING DATA

Sometimes you need to insert information into a worksheet right in the middle of existing data. Inserting cells causes the data in existing cells to shift down a row or over a column to create a space for the new cells.

> **Watch Your Formulas!** If your worksheet contains formulas that rely on the contents of the cells being shifted, the calculations may be thrown off. After inserting cells, double-check any formulas in your worksheet that might be affected.

To insert a single cell or a group of cells, follow these steps:

1. Select the area where you want the new cell inserted. Excel will insert the same number of cells as you select.

2. Open the Insert menu and choose Cells. The Insert dialog box appears.

3. Select Shift cells right or Shift cells down.

4. Click OK. Excel inserts the cell and shifts the data in the other cells in the specified direction. (See Figure 13.3.)

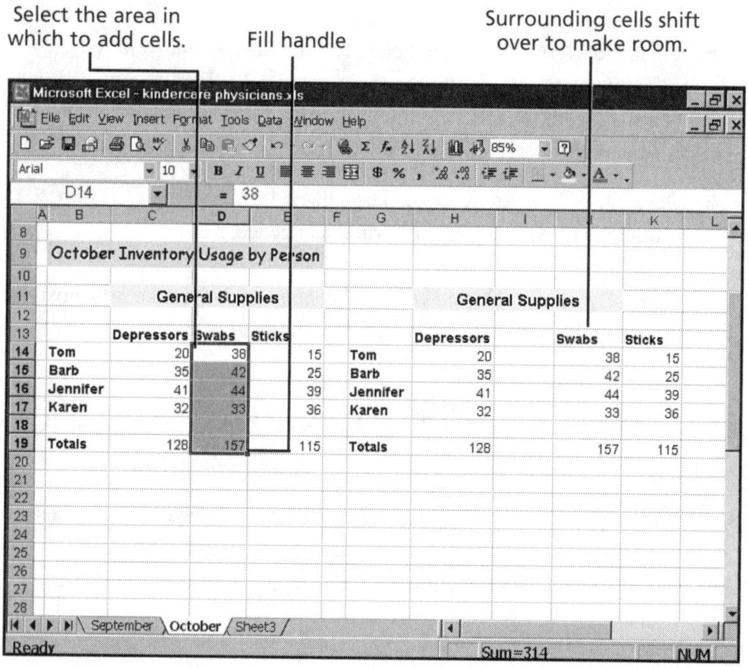

Select the area in which to add cells.   Fill handle   Surrounding cells shift over to make room.

FIGURE 13.3   Surrounding cells shift to make room for the new cells.

> **Drag Insert**   A quick way to insert cells is to select the number of cells you want, hold down the Shift key, and then drag the fill handle up, down, left, or right to set the position of the new cells. (The fill handle is the little box in the lower-right corner of the selected cell or cells (see Figure 13.3).

REMOVING CELLS BY SHIFTING DATA

In Lesson 12, you learned how to clear the contents and formatting of selected cells. That technique merely removed what was inside the cells. But you may want to eliminate the cells completely. When you do, Excel removes the cells and adjusts the data in surrounding cells to fill the gap.

If you want to remove the cells completely, perform the following steps:

1. Select the range of cells you want to remove.

2. Open the Edit menu and choose Delete. The Delete dialog box appears.

3. Select Shift cells left or Shift cells up.

4. Click OK. Surrounding cells are shifted to fill the gap left by the deleted cells.

In this lesson, you learned how to insert and delete cells, rows, and columns. In the next lesson, you will learn how to change the width and height of columns and rows.

LESSON 14

CHANGING COLUMN WIDTH AND ROW HEIGHT

In this lesson, you will learn how to adjust the width of your columns and the height of your rows to make the best use of the worksheet space.

ADJUSTING COLUMN WIDTH AND ROW HEIGHT WITH A MOUSE

You can adjust the width of a column or the height of a row by using a dialog box or by dragging with the mouse.

> **Why Bother?** You might not want to bother adjusting the row height because it's automatically adjusted as you change the size of text. However, if a column's width is not as large as its data, then the data might be displayed as ########. In such a case, you must adjust the width of the column in order for the data to be displayed at all.

Here's how you adjust the row height or column width with the mouse:

1. To change the height or width of two or more rows or columns, select them first by dragging over the row or column headings. To change a single column or row, skip this step and continue to step 2.

2. Position the mouse pointer over one of the row heading or column heading borders as shown in Figure 14.1. (Use the right border of the column heading to adjust column width; use the bottom border of the row heading to adjust the row height.)

3. Drag the border to the size you need it to be.

4. Release the mouse button, and Excel adjusts the row height or column width.

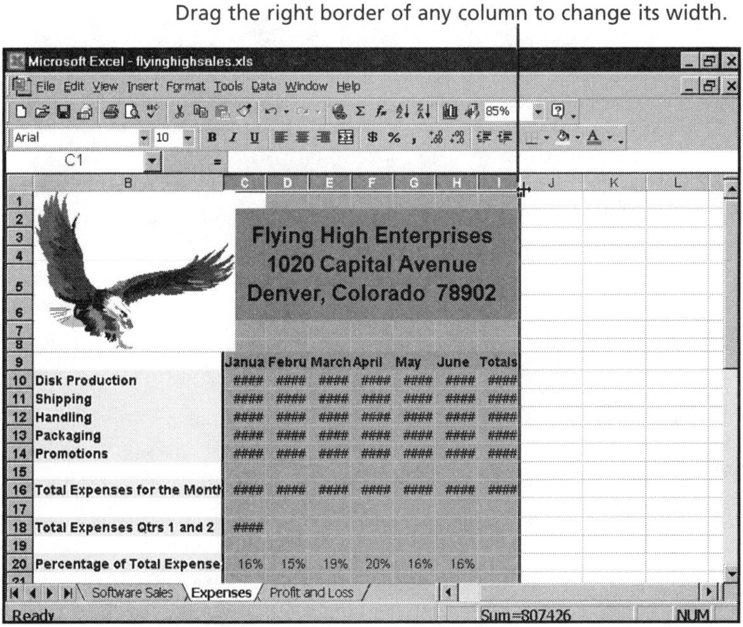

Drag the right border of any column to change its width.

FIGURE **14.1**   Resizing a column.

> **AutoFit Your Cells**   To quickly make a column as wide as its widest entry using Excel's AutoFit feature, double-click the right border of the column heading. To make a row as tall as its tallest entry, double-click on the bottom border of the row heading. To change more than one column or row at a time, drag over the desired row or column headings, and then double-click the bottommost or rightmost heading border.

USING THE FORMAT MENU FOR PRECISE CONTROL

You can change a column's size by dragging the border of a row or column. As you drag, a ScreenTip displays the current measurement of the column or row. Even so, you cannot control the size of your column or row as precisely as you can by entering specific sizes with a dialog box.

To change the column width or row height through a dialog box, follow these steps:

1. Select the column or row you want to change. To change the width of a single column or row, select any cell in that column/row.

2. Open the Format menu, select Column (or Row), and then select Width (or Height). A dialog box similar to the one shown in Figure 14.2 appears.

FIGURE **14.2**   Changing the column width.

3. Type the desired width (or height). When entering the width for a column, enter the *number of characters* you want the column's width to be. When entering the height of a row, enter the height you want *in points*.

4. Click OK or press Enter to put your changes into effect.

In this lesson, you learned how to change the row height and column width. In the next lesson, you will learn how to select, insert, delete, and move your worksheets.

LESSON 15

MANAGING
YOUR
WORKSHEETS

In this lesson, you learn how to add and delete worksheets within workbooks. You also learn how to copy, move, and rename worksheets.

SELECTING WORKSHEETS

By default, each workbook consists of three worksheets whose names appear on tabs at the bottom of the Excel window. You can add or delete worksheets as desired. One advantage to having multiple worksheets within a workbook is that it enables you to organize your data into logical chunks. Another advantage to having separate worksheets for your data is that you can reorganize the worksheets (and the associated data) in a workbook easily.

Before we go into the details of inserting, deleting, and copying worksheets, you should know how to select one or more worksheets. Here's what you need to know:

- To select a single worksheet, click its tab. The tab becomes highlighted to show that the worksheet is selected.

- To select several neighboring worksheets, click the tab of the first worksheet in the group, and then hold down the Shift key and click the tab of the last worksheet in the group.

- To select several non-neighboring worksheets, hold down the Ctrl key and click each worksheet's tab.

If you select two or more worksheets, they remain selected until you ungroup them. To ungroup worksheets, do one of the following:

- Right-click one of the selected worksheets and choose Ungroup Sheets.

- Hold down the Shift key and click the tab of the active worksheet.

- Click any tab.

INSERTING WORKSHEETS

When you create a new workbook, it contains three worksheets. You can easily add additional worksheets to a workbook.

Follow these steps to add a worksheet to a workbook:

1. Select the worksheet *before* which you want the new worksheet inserted. For example, if you select Sheet2, the new worksheet (which will be called Sheet4 because the workbook already contains three worksheets) will be inserted *before* Sheet2.

2. Open the Insert menu.

3. Select Worksheet. Excel inserts the new worksheet, as shown in Figure 15.1.

> **Shortcut Menu**   A faster way to work with worksheets is to right-click the worksheet tab. This brings up a shortcut menu that lets you insert, delete, rename, move, copy, or select all worksheets.

> **Start with More**   You can change the number of worksheets Excel places in a new workbook by opening the Tools menu, selecting Options, clicking the General tab, and then changing the number in the Sheets in new workbook option. Click OK to save your changes.

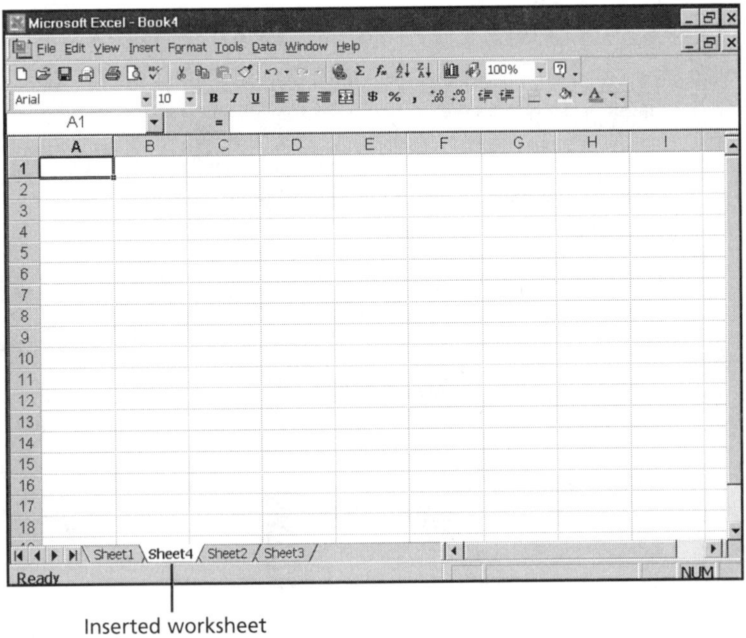

Inserted worksheet

FIGURE **15.1**   Excel inserts the new worksheet before the active worksheet.

DELETING WORKSHEETS

If you plan to use only one worksheet, you can remove the two other worksheets. Here's how you remove a worksheet:

1. Select the worksheet you want to delete.

2. Open the Edit menu.

3. Click Delete Sheet. A dialog box appears, asking you to confirm the deletion.

You Could Lose Data, Too!   If the worksheet you selected contains any data, you'll lose the data as well, so be careful when deleting worksheets.

4. Click the OK button. The worksheet is deleted.

MOVING AND COPYING WORKSHEETS

You can move or copy worksheets within a workbook or from one work-book to another. Here's how:

1. Select the worksheet you want to move or copy. If you want to move or copy worksheets from one workbook to another, be sure to open the target workbook.

2. Open the Edit menu and choose Move or Copy Sheet. The Move or Copy dialog box appears, as shown in Figure 15.2.

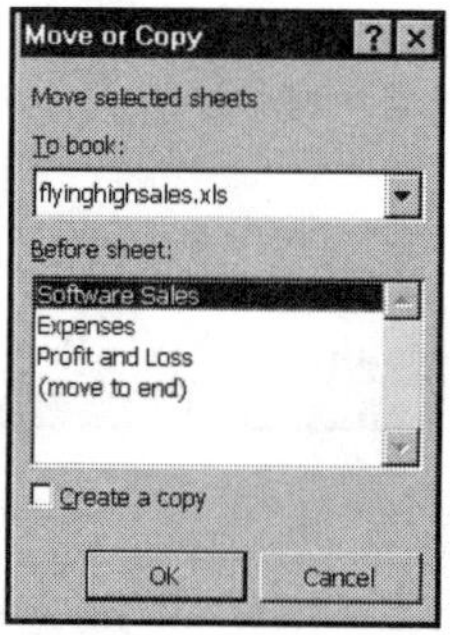

FIGURE **15.2**   The Move or Copy dialog box asks where you want to copy or move a worksheet.

3. To move the worksheet to a different workbook, make sure that workbook is open, then select that workbook's name from the To book drop-down list. If you want to move or copy the worksheet to a new workbook, select (new book) in the To book drop-down list. Excel creates a new workbook and then copies or moves the worksheet to it.

4. In the Before sheet list box, choose the worksheet *before* which you want the selected worksheet to be moved.

5. To copy the selected worksheet instead of moving it, select the Create a copy option.

6. Select OK. The selected worksheets are copied or moved as specified.

MOVING A WORKSHEET WITHIN A WORKBOOK BY DRAGGING AND DROPPING

An easier way to copy or move worksheets within a workbook is to use drag and drop. First, select the tab of the worksheet you want to copy or move. Move the mouse pointer over one of the selected tabs, click and hold the mouse button, and drag the tab to where you want it moved. To copy the worksheet, hold down the Ctrl key while dragging. When you release the mouse button, the worksheet is copied or moved.

MOVING A WORKSHEET BETWEEN WORKBOOKS BY DRAGGING AND DROPPING

You can also use the drag and drop feature to quickly copy or move worksheets between workbooks. First, open the workbooks you want to use for the copy or move. Choose Window, Arrange and select the Tiled option. Click OK to arrange the windows so that a small portion of each one appears onscreen. Select the tab of the worksheet you want to copy or move. Move the mouse pointer over one of the selected tabs, click and hold the mouse button, and drag the tab where you want it moved. To copy the worksheet, hold down the Ctrl key while dragging. When you release the mouse button, the worksheet is copied or moved.

CHANGING WORKSHEET TAB NAMES

By default, all worksheets are named "SheetX," where X is a number starting with the number 1. So that you'll have a better idea of the information each sheet contains, you should change the names that appear on the tabs. Here's how to do it:

1. Double-click the tab of the worksheet you want to rename. The current name is highlighted.

2. Type a new name for the worksheet and press Enter. Excel replaces the default name with the name you typed.

In this lesson, you learned how to insert, delete, move, copy, and rename worksheets. In the next lesson, you'll learn how to print your workbook.

LESSON 16

PRINTING YOUR WORKBOOK

In this lesson, you will learn how to print an entire workbook or a portion of it.

CHANGING THE PAGE SETUP

A *workbook* is a collection of many worksheets, which are like pages in a notebook. You can print the whole workbook at once, or just one or more pages (one or more worksheets) at a time. When you print a worksheet, if it contains a chart, the chart will be printed as well (you'll learn how to create charts in Lesson 24).

Before you print a worksheet, you should make sure that the page is set up correctly for printing. To do this, open the File menu and choose Page Setup. You'll see the Page Setup dialog box shown in Figure 16.1.

FIGURE 16.1 The Page Setup dialog box.

> **Click That Control Box!** For quick access to commands that affect a workbook, just right-click the workbook's control box (it's to the left of the File menu). For example, to check the page setup, right-click the **Control box** and choose **Page Setup**.

The following list outlines the page setup settings, grouped according to the tab on which they appear.

Page tab

> **Orientation.** Select Portrait to print across the short edge of a page; select Landscape to print across the long edge of a page. (Landscape makes the page wider than it is tall.)
>
> **Scaling.** You can reduce and enlarge your workbook or force it to fit within a specific page size (see Lesson 17).
>
> **Paper size.** This is set to 8 1/2 by 11 inches by default, but you can choose a different size from the list.
>
> **Print quality.** You can print your spreadsheet in draft quality to print quickly and save wear and tear on your printer, or you can print in high quality for a final copy. Print quality is measured in dpi (dots per inch); the higher the number, the better the print quality.
>
> **First page number.** You can set the starting page number to something other than 1. The Auto option (default) tells Excel to set the starting page number to 1 if it is the first page in the print job, or to set the first page number to the next sequential number if it is not the first page in the print job.

Margins tab

> **Top, Bottom, Left, Right.** You can adjust the size of the top, bottom, left, and right margins.
>
> **Header, Footer.** You can specify how far you want a Header or Footer printed from the edge of the page. (You use the Header/ Footer tab to add a header or footer to your workbook—see Lesson 17 for help.)

Center on page. You can center your workbook data between the left and right margins (Horizontally) and between the top and bottom margins (Vertically).

Header/Footer tab

Header, Footer. You can add a header (such as a title) that repeats at the top of each page, or a footer (such as page numbers) that repeats at the bottom of each page. See Lesson 17 for more information on headers and footers.

Custom Header, Custom Footer. You can use the Custom Header or Custom Footer button to create headers and footers that insert the time, date, worksheet tab name, and workbook file name.

Sheet tab

Print area. You can print a portion of a workbook or worksheet by entering the range of cells you want to print. You can type the range, or click the Collapse Dialog button at the right of the text box to move the Page Setup dialog box out of the way and drag the mouse pointer over the desired cells (see Lesson 17). If you do not select a print area, Excel will print either the sheet or the workbook, depending on the options set in the Page tab.

Don't Print That!   Ordinarily, if there's a portion of your worksheet that you don't want to print, you can avoid it by selecting the area you want to print and printing only that selection. However, if the data you want to hide is located *within* the area you want to print, what do you do? In that case, you hide the columns, rows, or cells to prevent them from being printed. (See Lesson 8 for help.)

Print titles. If you have a row or column of entries that you want repeated as titles on every page, type the range for this row or column, or drag over the cells with the mouse pointer.

Print. You can tell Excel exactly how to print some aspects of the workbook. For example, you can have the gridlines (the lines that define the cells) printed. You can also have a color spreadsheet printed in black and white.

Page order. You can indicate how data in the worksheet should be read and printed: in sections from top to bottom or in sections from left to right. This is the way Excel handles printing the areas outside of the printable area. For example, if some columns to the right don't fit on the first page and some rows don't fit at the bottom of the first page, you can specify which area will print next.

When you finish entering your settings, click the OK button.

PREVIEWING A PRINT JOB

After you've determined your page setup and print area, you should preview what the printed page will look like before you print. That way, if the worksheet needs to be adjusted, or if there are any page setup changes you would like to make, you can do so without wasting any paper. To preview a print job, open the File menu and select Print Preview, or click the Print Preview button in the Standard toolbar. Your workbook appears as it will when printed, as shown in Figure 16.2.

 Another Print Preview   You can also preview a print job when you are setting up a page or while you are in the Page Setup dialog box. When the Page Setup dialog box is displayed, click the Print Preview button. In the Print dialog box, click the Preview button to preview a worksheet.

A Close-Up View   Zoom in on any area of the preview by clicking on it with the mouse pointer (which looks like a magnifying glass). You can also use the Zoom button at the top of the Print Preview screen.

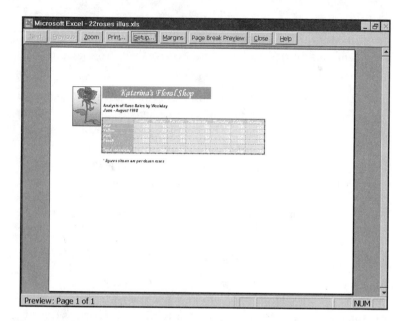

FIGURE 16.2   By previewing the worksheet, you can tell whether you need to change to landscape orientation.

PRINTING YOUR WORKBOOK

After adjusting the page settings and previewing your data, it is time to print. You can print selected data, selected sheets, or the entire workbook.

To print your workbook, follow these steps:

1. If you want to print a portion of the worksheet, select the range you want to print (see Lesson 11 for help). To print just a chart, click on it. If you want to print one or more worksheets within the workbook, select the sheet tabs (see Lesson 15). To print the entire workbook, skip this step.

2. Open the File menu and select Print (or press Ctrl+P). The Print dialog box appears, as shown in Figure 16.3.

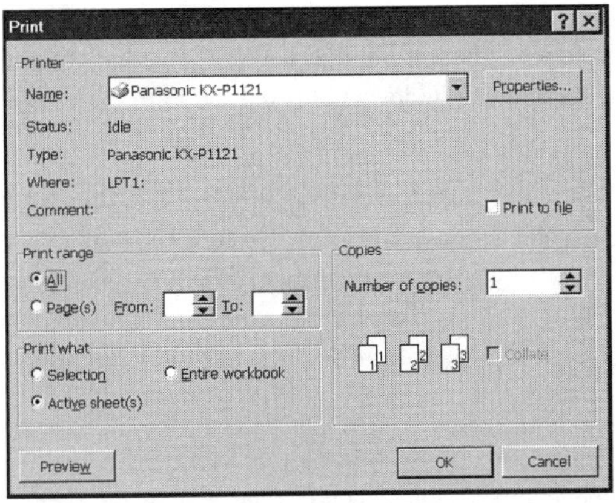

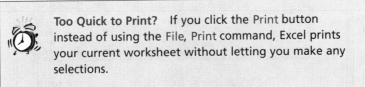

FIGURE **16.3** The Print dialog box.

Too Quick to Print? If you click the Print button instead of using the File, Print command, Excel prints your current worksheet without letting you make any selections.

---

3. Select the options you would like to use:

Print range lets you print one or more pages. For example, if the selected print area contains 15 pages and you want to print only pages 5–10, select Pages, and then type the numbers of the first and last page you want to print in the from and to boxes.

Print what enables you to print the currently selected cells, the selected worksheets, or the entire workbook.

Copies enables you to print more than one copy of the selection, worksheet, or workbook.

Collate enables you to print a complete copy of the selection, worksheet, or workbook before the first page of the next copy is printed. This option is available when you print multiple copies.

4. Click OK or press Enter.

While your job is printing, you can continue working in Excel. If the printer is working on another job that you (or someone else, in the case of a network printer) sent, Windows holds the job until the printer is ready for it.

Sometimes you might want to delete a job while it is printing or before it prints. For example, suppose you think of other numbers to add to the worksheet or realize you forgot to format some text; you'll want to fix these things before you print the file. In such a case, deleting the print job is easy. To display the print queue and delete a print job, follow these steps:

1. Double-click the Printer icon on the Windows taskbar, and the print queue appears, as shown in Figure 16.4.

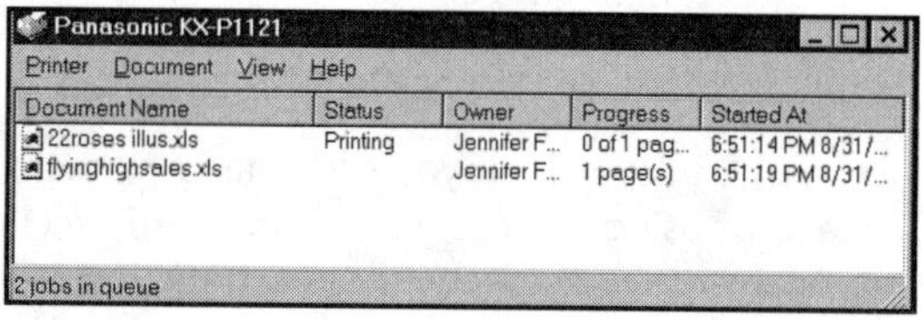

FIGURE 16.4   To stop a document from printing, use the print queue.

2. Click on the job you want to delete.

3. Open the Document menu and select Cancel Printing or just press Delete.

To delete all the files from the print queue, open the Printer menu and select Purge Print Documents. This cancels the print jobs, but doesn't delete the files from your computer.

> **Send a Worksheet to a Colleague**   Instead of printing your worksheet, why not send it directly to the people who need it? Open the File menu, select Send To, and then select the appropriate option: Mail Recipient (as Attachment) (to send a workbook as an attachment to an email message), Routing Recipient (route a workbook over a local network through Microsoft Mail or cc:Mail to several people), Exchange Folder (to post (copy) your workbook to a Microsoft Exchange server), or Online Meeting Participant (to send the workbook to a person with whom you are having an online meeting). You can also use the E-Mail button on the Standard toolbar to email a worksheet.

In this lesson, you learned how to print all or part of your workbook. In the next lesson, you will learn how to print large worksheets.

LESSON 17

PRINTING LARGE WORKSHEETS

In this lesson, you will learn about the many aspects involved in printing a large worksheet.

SELECTING A PRINT AREA

You do not always have to print an entire worksheet; instead, you can easily tell Excel what part of the worksheet you want to print by selecting the print area yourself. If the area you select is too large to fit on one page, no problem—Excel just breaks it into multiple pages. When you do not select a print area yourself, Excel prints either the entire worksheet or the entire workbook, depending on the options set in the Print dialog box.

 Double Vision! When deciding which cells to select for your print area, make sure you *do not include the title, the subtitle, and the column and row labels in the print area.* If you do, Excel may print the labels twice. Instead, print your titles and headings on each page of your printout by following the steps in the upcoming section, "Printing Column and Row Labels."

To select a print area:

1. Click on the upper-left cell of the range you want to print.

2. Drag downward and to the right until the range you want is selected.

3. Open the File menu, select Print Area, and select Set Print Area.

To remove the print area so you can print the entire worksheet again, open the File menu, select Print Area, and select Clear Print Area.

You can also select your print area from within the Page Setup dialog box, shown in Figure 17.1. First, open the File menu and select Page Setup. Click the Sheet tab, then click the Collapse Dialog button to the right of the Print Area text box. Select the range you want to print, then click the Collapse Dialog button again to return to the Page Setup dialog box. Make any other changes you want, and click Print.

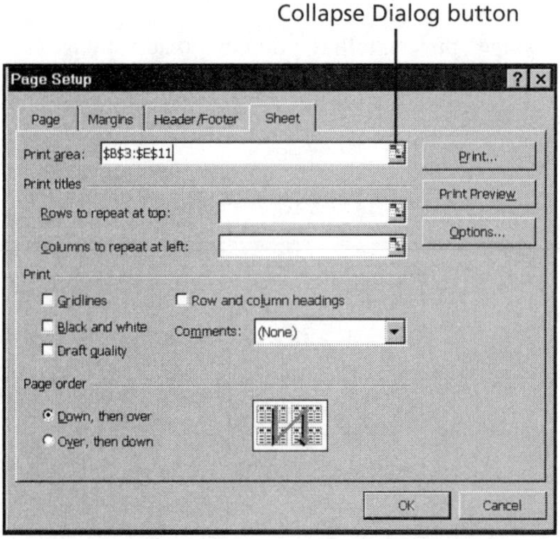

Collapse Dialog button

FIGURE 17.1 It's easy to select a print area from within the Page Setup dialog box.

ADJUSTING PAGE BREAKS

When you print a workbook, Excel determines the page breaks based on the paper size and margins and the selected print area. To make the pages look better and break information in logical places, you may want to override the automatic page breaks with your own breaks. However, before you add page breaks, try these options:

- Adjust the widths of individual columns to make the best use of space (see Lesson 14).

- Consider printing the workbook sideways (using Landscape orientation)—see Lesson 16.

- Change the left, right, top, and bottom margins to smaller values—again, see Lesson 16 for help.

If after trying these options you still want to insert page breaks, Excel offers you an option of previewing exactly where the page breaks appear and then adjusting them. Follow these steps:

1. Open the **View** menu and select **Page Break Preview**.

2. If a message appears, telling you how to adjust page breaks, click **OK**. Your worksheet is displayed with page breaks, as shown in Figure 17.2.

Drag a page break to adjust its position.

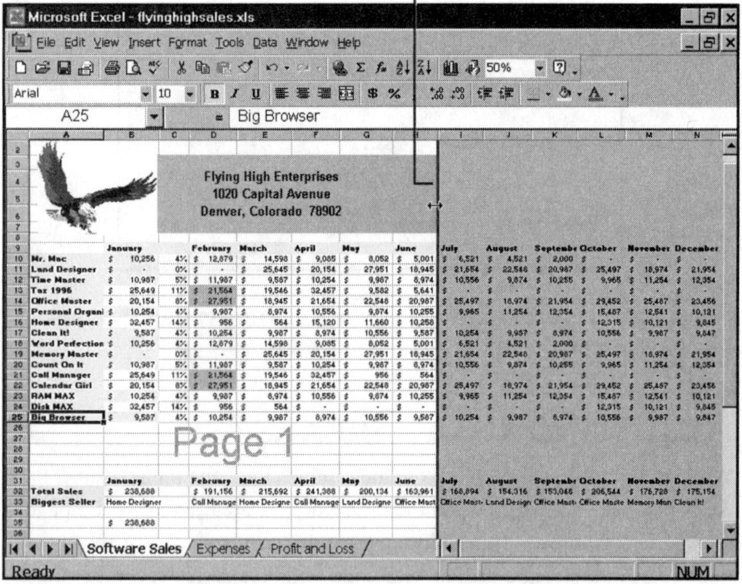

FIGURE **17.2**   Check your page breaks before printing your worksheet.

3. To move a page break, drag the blue line to the desired location.

   To delete a page break, drag it off the screen.

   To insert a page break, move to the first cell in the column to the right of where you want the page break inserted, or move to the row below where you want the break inserted. For example, to insert a page break between columns G and H, move to cell H1. To insert a page break between rows 24 and 25, move to cell A25. Then open the Insert menu and select Page Break. A dashed line appears to the left of the selected column or above the selected row.

4. To exit Page Break Preview and return to your normal worksheet view, open the View menu and select Normal.

PRINTING COLUMN AND ROW LABELS ON EVERY PAGE

Excel provides a way for you to select labels and titles that are located on the top edge and left side of a large worksheet, and print them on every page of the printout. This option is useful when a worksheet is too wide to print on a single page. If you don't use this option, the extra columns or rows will be printed on subsequent pages without any descriptive labels.

Follow these steps to print column or row labels on every page:

1. Open the File menu and choose Page Setup. The Page Setup dialog box appears.

2. Click the Sheet tab to display the Sheet options.

3. To repeat column labels and a worksheet title, click the Collapse Dialog button to the right of the Rows to repeat at top text box.

4. Drag over the rows you want to print on every page, as shown in Figure 17.3. A dashed line border surrounds the selected area, and absolute cell references with dollar signs appear in the Rows to repeat at top text box.

Select the rows
you want to repeat.   Collapse Dialog button

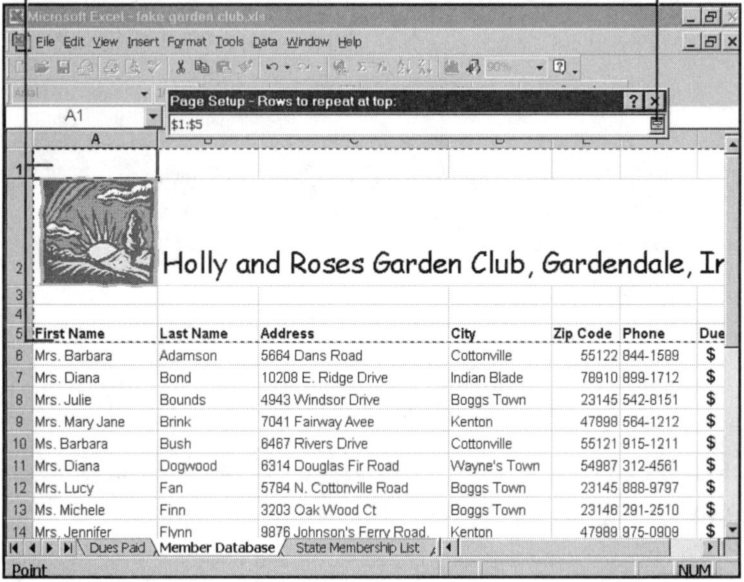

FIGURE **17.3**   Select the headings you want to print on every page.

5. Click the Collapse Dialog button to return to the Page Setup dialog box.

6. To repeat row labels that appear on the left of the worksheet, click the Collapse Dialog button to the right of the Columns to repeat at left text box. Excel reduces the Page Setup dialog box.

7. Select the columns that contain the row labels you want to repeat.

8. Click the Collapse Dialog button to return once again to the Page Setup dialog box.

9. To print your worksheet, click Print to display the Print dialog box. Then click OK.

Select Your Print Area Carefully   If you select rows or columns to repeat, and those rows or columns are part of your print area, the selected rows or columns may print twice. To fix this, select your print area again, leaving out the rows or columns you're repeating. See "Selecting a Print Area" earlier in this lesson for help.

ADDING HEADERS AND FOOTERS

Excel lets you add headers and footers to print information at the top and bottom of every page of the printout. The information can include any text, as well as page numbers, the current date and time, the workbook file name, and the worksheet tab name.

You can choose the headers and footers suggested by Excel, or you can include any text plus special commands to control the appearance of the header or footer. For example, you can apply bold, italic, or underline to the header or footer text. You can also left-align, center, or right-align your text in a header or footer (see Lesson 22).

To add headers and footers, follow these steps:

1. Open the View menu and choose Header and Footer. The Page Setup dialog box appears (see Figure 17.4).

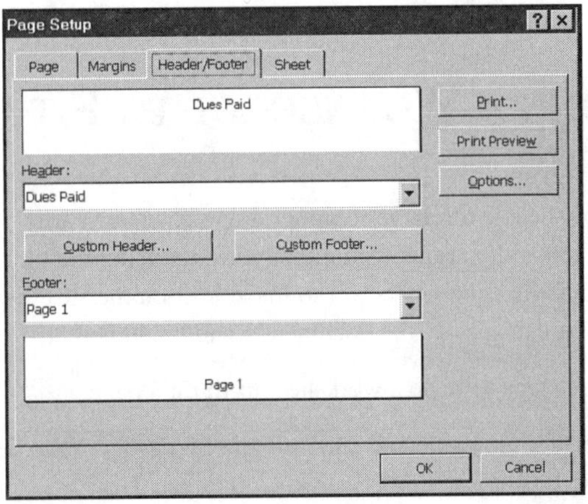

FIGURE 17.4   Adding headers and footers with Header/Footer options.

2. To select a header, click the Header drop-down arrow. Excel displays a list of suggested header information. Scroll through the list and click the header you want. The sample header appears at the top of the Header/Footer tab.

Don't See One You Like?   If none of the suggested headers or footers suit you, click the **Custom Header** or **Custom Footer** button and enter your own information.

3. To select a footer, click the Footer drop-down arrow. Excel displays a list of suggested footer information. Scroll through the list and click on a footer you want. The sample footer appears at the bottom of the Header/Footer tab.

4. Click OK to close the Page Setup dialog box and return to your worksheet. Or click the Print button to display the Print dialog box, and click OK to print your worksheet.

Don't Want Headers or Footers Anymore?   To remove the header and/or footer, choose (none) in the Header and/or Footer lists.

SCALING A WORKSHEET TO FIT ON A PAGE

If your worksheet is too large to print on one page even after you change the orientation and margins, you might consider using the Fit to option. This option shrinks the worksheet to make it fit on the specified number of pages. You can specify the document's width and height.

Follow these steps to scale a worksheet to fit on a page:

1. Open the File menu and choose Page Setup. The Page Setup dialog box appears.

2. Click the Page tab to display the Page options.

3. In the Fit to XX page wide by XX tall text boxes, enter the number of pages in which you want Excel to fit your data.

4. Click OK to close the Page Setup dialog box and return to your worksheet. Or click the Print button in the Page Setup dialog box to display the Print dialog box, and then click OK to print your worksheet.

In this lesson, you learned how to print a large worksheet. In the next lesson, you will learn how to create calculations in your worksheet.

Lesson 18

Performing Calculations With Formulas

In this lesson, you will learn how to use formulas to calculate results in your worksheets.

Understanding Excel Formulas

You can use Excel formulas to perform simple calculations on the data you enter. With formulas, you can perform addition, subtraction, multiplication, and division using the values contained in various cells.

Formulas typically consist of one or more cell addresses or values and a mathematical operator, such as + (addition), – (subtraction), * (multiplication), or / (division). For example, if you want to determine the average of the three values contained in cells A1, B1, and C1, you would type the following formula in the cell where you want the result to appear:

`=(A1+B1+C1)/3`

 Start Right Every formula must begin with an equal sign (=). If you don't type an = when you enter a formula, Excel may interpret what you type as a date or a label.

Figure 18.1 shows several formulas in action. Study the formulas and their results. Table 18.1 lists the mathematical operators you can use to create formulas.

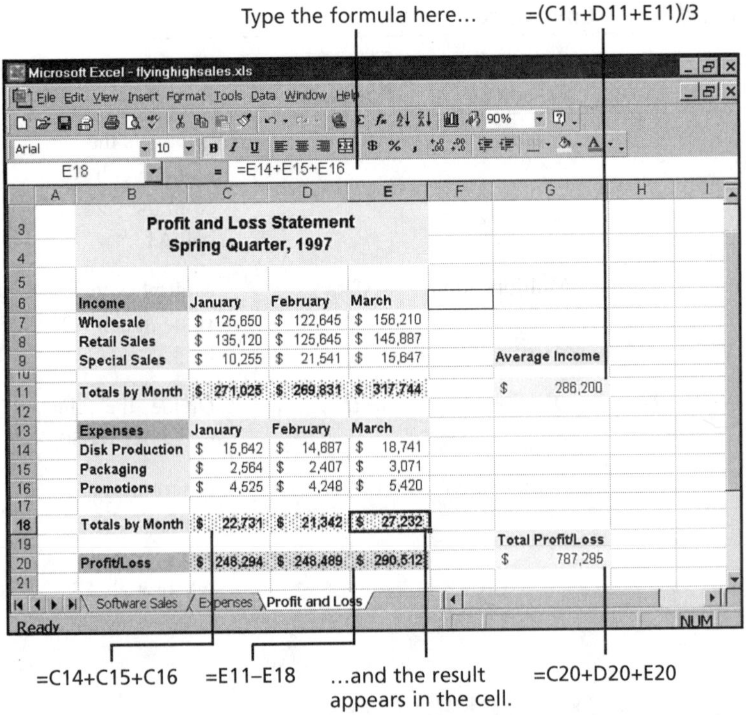

Type the formula here...   =(C11+D11+E11)/3

=C14+C15+C16   =E11–E18   ...and the result   =C20+D20+E20
appears in the cell.

FIGURE **18.1** Type a formula in the cell where you want the result to appear.

TABLE **18.1** EXCEL'S MATHEMATICAL OPERATORS

OPERATOR	PERFORMS	SAMPLE FORMULA	RESULT
^	Exponentiation	=A1^3	Enters the result of raising the value in cell A1 to the third power.
+	Addition	=A1+A2	Enters the total of the values in cells A1 and A2.

continues

TABLE 18.1   CONTINUED

OPERATOR	PERFORMS	SAMPLE FORMULA	RESULT
–	Subtraction	=A1–A2	Subtracts the value in cell A2 from the value in cell A1.
*	Multiplication	=A2*3	Multiplies the value in cell A2 by 3.
/	Division	=A1/50	Divides the value in cell A1 by 50.
	Combination	=(A1+A2+A3)/3	Determines the average of the values in cells A1 through A3.

ORDER OF OPERATIONS

Excel performs the operations within a formula in the following order:

1st   Exponential and equations within parentheses

2nd   Multiplication and division

3rd   Addition and subtraction

For example, given the formula =C2+B8*4+D10, Excel computes the value of B8*4, then adds that to C2, and then adds D10. Keep this order of operations in mind when you are creating equations because it determines the result.

If you don't take this order into consideration, you could run into problems when entering your formulas. For example, if you want to determine the average of the values in cells A1, B1, and C1, and you enter =A1+B1+C1/3, you'll get the wrong answer. The value in C1 will be divided by 3, and that result will be added to A1+B1. To determine the total of A1 through C1 first, you must enclose that group of values in parentheses: =(A1+B1+C1)/3.

ENTERING FORMULAS

You can enter formulas in either of two ways: by typing the formula or by selecting cell references.

To type a formula, perform the following steps:

1. Select the cell in which you want the formula's calculation to appear.

2. Type the equal sign (=), or click the Equal button.

3. Type the formula. The formula appears in the Formula bar.

4. Press Enter or click the Enter button on the Formula bar, and Excel calculates the result.

> **Unwanted Formula**   If you start to enter a formula and then decide you don't want to use it, you can skip entering the formula by pressing Esc or clicking the Cancel button on the Formula bar.

> **Name That Cell**   If you plan to use a particular cell in several formulas, you can give it a name, such as "Income." Then you can use the name in the formula, as in =Income+$12.50. To name a cell, use the Insert, Name, Define command.

To enter a formula by selecting cell references, take the following steps:

1. Select the cell in which you want the formula's result to appear.

2. Type the equal sign (=) or click the Equal button.

3. Click the cell whose address you want to appear first in the formula. You can also click on a cell in a different worksheet or workbook. The cell address appears in the Formula bar.

4. Type a mathematical operator after the value to indicate the next operation you want to perform. The operator appears in the Formula bar.

5. Continue clicking cells and typing operators until the formula is complete.

6. Press Enter or click the Enter button on the Formula bar to accept the formula, or press Esc or click to cancel the operation.

Error! If ERR appears in a cell, make sure that you did not commit one of these common errors: dividing by zero, using a blank cell as a divisor, referring to a blank cell, deleting a cell used in a formula, or including a reference to the cell in which the answer appears.

Natural Language Formulas Excel lets you refer to row and column labels when entering a formula. For example, if you had a worksheet with the row labels "Revenues," "Expenses," and "Profit," and you had column labels for each month, you could enter a formula such as =Jan Profit+Feb Profit or =Revenues–Expenses.

CALCULATING RESULTS WITHOUT ENTERING A FORMULA

Using AutoCalculate, you can view the sum of a range of cells by selecting the cells and looking at the status bar (see Figure 18.2). You can also view the average, minimum, maximum, and the count of a range of cells. To display something other than the sum, right-click the status bar and select the option from the shortcut menu that appears.

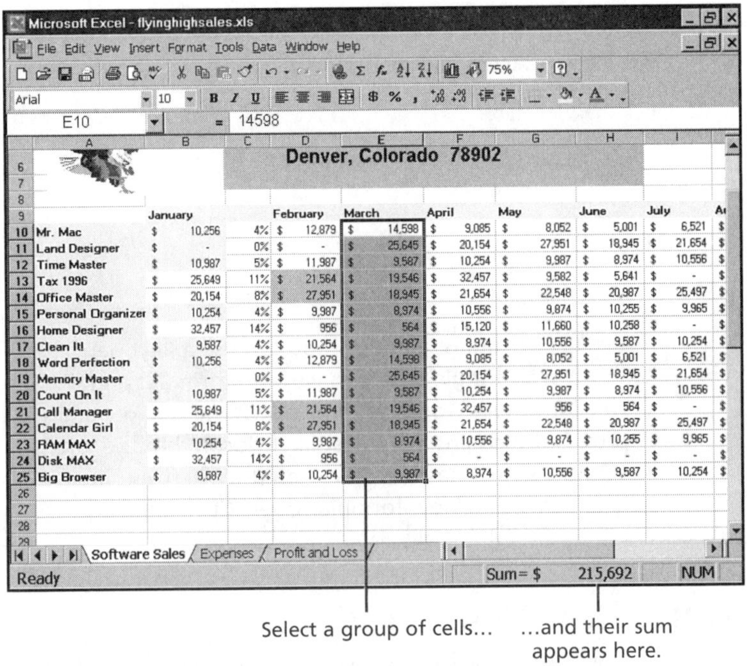

Select a group of cells...   ...and their sum
appears here.

FIGURE 18.2   View a sum without entering a formula.

> **Where's the Status Bar?**   If the status bar is not visible on your screen, you can display it by opening the View menu and place a check next to it by clicking Status Bar.

DISPLAYING FORMULAS

Normally, Excel does not display the actual formula in a cell. Instead, it displays the result of the calculation. You can view the formula by selecting the cell and looking in the Formula bar. However, if you're trying to review all the formulas in a large worksheet, it would be easier if you could see them all at once (and even print them).

If you want to view formulas in a worksheet, follow these steps:

1. Open the Tools menu and choose Options.

2. Click the View tab.

3. In the Window Options area, click to select the Formulas check box.

4. Click OK.

Display Formulas Quickly   You can use a keyboard shortcut to toggle between viewing formulas and viewing values. To do so, hold down the Ctrl key and press `, the accent key (most likely located to the left of the 1 key; it has the tilde ~ on it). When you no longer need to view formulas, press Ctrl+` again.

EDITING FORMULAS

Editing a formula is the same as editing any entry in Excel. Here's how you do it:

1. Select the cell that contains the formula you want to edit.

2. Click in the Formula bar or press F2 to enter Edit mode.

Quick In-Cell Editing   To quickly edit the contents of a cell, double-click the cell. The insertion point appears inside the cell, and you can make any necessary changes.

---

3. Press the left arrow key ← or right arrow → key to move the insertion point. Then use the Backspace key to delete characters to the left, or use the Delete key to delete characters to the right. Type any additional characters.

4. When you finish editing the data, click the Enter button on the Formula bar or press Enter to accept your changes.

Another way to edit a formula is to click the Edit Formula button on the Formula bar. When you do, the Formula bar expands to provide you with help. Make your changes to the formula and then click OK.

In this lesson, you learned how to enter and edit formulas. In the next lesson, you will learn how to copy formulas, when to use relative and absolute cell addresses, and how to change Excel's settings for calculating formulas in the worksheet.

LESSON 19

COPYING FORMULAS AND RECALCULATING

In this lesson, you will learn how to copy formulas, use relative and absolute cell references, and change calculation settings.

COPYING FORMULAS

When you copy a formula, the formula is adjusted to fit the location of the cell to which it is copied. This is called *relative addressing,* because the addresses of the cells in the original formula are adjusted to reflect their new column or row. For example, if you copy the formula =C2+C3 from cell C4 to cell D4 (a different column), the formula is adjusted to column D: it becomes =D2+D3. This allows you to copy a formula (such as one that totals monthly expenses for January) to a range of cells (such as the February, March, and April columns).

You can copy formulas using the Copy and Paste buttons (see Lesson 12), but there's a faster way:

1. Click the cell that contains the formula you want to copy.

2. Press Ctrl and drag the cell's border to the cell to which you want to copy your formula.

3. Release the mouse button, and Excel copies the formula to the new location.

If you want to copy a formula to a neighboring range of cells, follow these steps:

1. Click the cell that contains the formula you want to copy.

2. Move the mouse pointer over the fill handle.

3. Drag the fill handle across the cells into which you want to copy the formula.

> **Fast Copy**   If you want to enter the same formula into a range of cells, select the range first. Then type the formula for the first cell in the range and press Ctrl+Enter.

> **Get an Error?**   If you get an error after copying a formula, verify the cell references in the copied formula. See the next section, "Using Relative and Absolute Cell Addresses," for more details.

USING RELATIVE AND ABSOLUTE CELL ADDRESSES

As I mentioned at the beginning of this lesson, when you copy a formula from one place in the worksheet to another, Excel adjusts the cell references in the formulas relative to their new positions in the worksheet. For example, in Figure 19.1, cell C16 contains the formula =C10+C11+C12+C13+C14, which computes the total expenses for January. If you copy that formula to cell D16 (to determine the total expenses for February), Excel automatically changes the formula to =D10+D11+D12+D13+D14. Because you copied the formula to a different column (from C to D), Excel adjusts the column letter in the cell addresses. If you had copied the same formula to cell C18 (two rows down), then the formula would be changed to =C12+C13+C14+C15+C16; all the cell addresses would be adjusted by two rows. This is how relative cell addresses work.

Sometimes you may not want the cell references to be adjusted when you copy formulas. That's when absolute cell references become important.

In the example shown in Figure 19.1, the formulas in cells C20, D20, E20, and F20 contain formulas that calculate the percentage of total expenses for that month. Each formula uses an absolute reference to cell C18, which contains the total expenses for quarters 1 and 2. (The formulas in C20, D20, E20, and F20 divide the sums from row 16 of each column by the contents of cell C18.) If you didn't use an absolute reference when you copied the formula from C20 to the range D20:F20, the cell references would be incorrect, and you would get an error message.

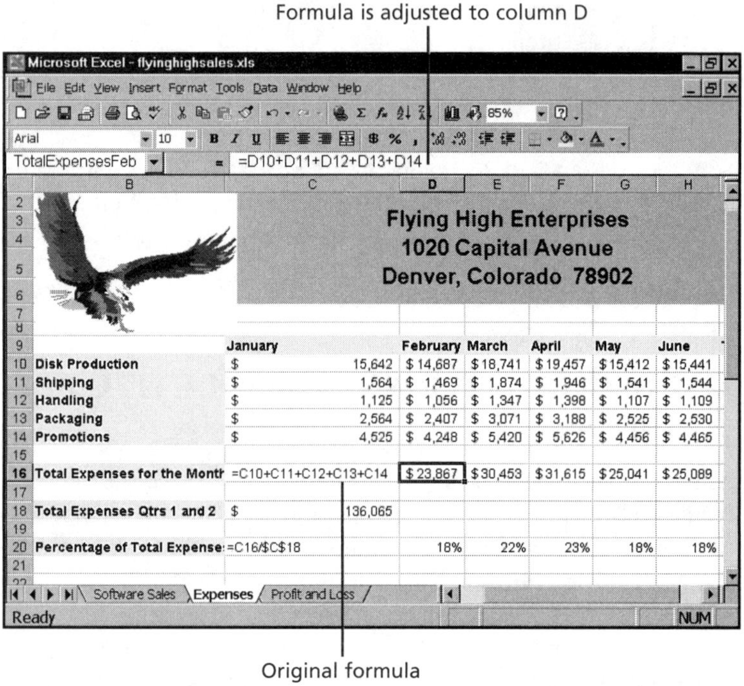

Formula is adjusted to column D

Original formula

FIGURE 19.1   Excel adjusts cell references when you copy formulas to different cells.

> **Absolute Versus Relative**   An *absolute reference* is a cell reference in a formula that does not change when copied to a new location. A *relative reference* is a cell reference in a formula that is adjusted when the formula is copied.

To make a cell reference in a formula absolute, you add a $ (dollar sign) before the letter and before the number that make up the cell address. For example, in Figure 19.1, the formula in C20 reads as follows:

```
=C16/$C$18
```

The address, $C$18 refers to cell C18, which contains the total expenses for quarters 1 and 2. When you copy this formula to column D, it becomes:

`=D16/$C$18`

If you hadn't used absolute cell references, the formula would have changed to =D16/D18. Since cell D18 is empty, the formula would have resulted in an error. To enter absolute cell addresses, you can type the dollar signs yourself, or just press F4 after typing the cell address.

Some formulas use mixed references. For example, the column letter might be an absolute reference, and the row number might be a relative reference, as in the formula $A2/2. If you entered this formula in cell C2 and then copied it to cell D10 (one column over and eight rows down), the result would be the formula $A10/2. The row reference (row number) would be adjusted by eight rows, but the column reference (the letter A) would not be adjusted at all.

 Mixed References   A reference that is only partially absolute, such as A$2 or $A2. When a formula that uses a mixed reference is copied to another cell, only part of the cell reference (the relative part) is adjusted.

CONTROLLING WHEN YOUR WORKSHEET IS RECALCULATED

Excel recalculates the formulas in a worksheet every time you edit a value in a cell. However, on a large worksheet, you may not want Excel to recalculate until you have entered all of your changes. For example, if you are entering a lot of changes to a worksheet that contains many formulas, you can speed up the process by changing from automatic to manual recalculation. To change the recalculation setting, take the following steps:

1. Open the Tools menu and choose Options.

2. Click the Calculation tab to display the options shown in Figure 19.2.

3. Select one of the following Calculation options:

> **Automatic.** This is the default setting. It recalculates the entire workbook each time you edit or enter a formula.

> **Automatic except tables.** This automatically recalculates everything except formulas in a data table. You'll learn about data tables (databases) in Lesson 28.

> **Manual.** This option tells Excel to recalculate only when you say so. To recalculate using this option, you press **F9** or choose Tools, Options, Calculation and click the Calc Now (F9) button. When this option is selected, you can turn the Recalculate before save option off or on.

4. Click OK.

Select to perform manual calculations.

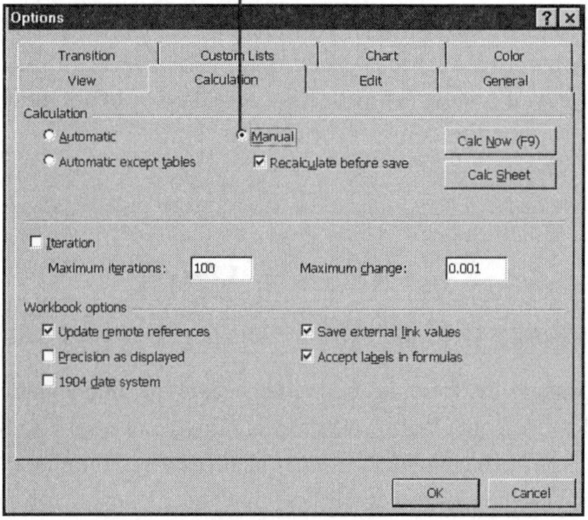

FIGURE 19.2   Change your calculation setting in the Options dialog box.

In this lesson, you learned how to copy formulas. You also learned when to use relative and absolute cell addresses and how to change recalculation settings. In the next lesson, you will learn how to use Excel's Function Wizard to insert another type of formula called a function.

LESSON 20

PERFORMING CALCULATIONS WITH FUNCTIONS

In this lesson, you will learn how to perform calculations with functions and how to use Excel's Function Wizard to quickly insert functions in cells.

WHAT ARE FUNCTIONS?

Functions are complex ready-made formulas that perform a series of operations on a specified range of values. For example, to determine the sum of a series of numbers in cells A1 through H1, you can enter the function =SUM(A1:H1) instead of entering =A1+B1+C1 and so on.

Every function consists of the following three elements:

- The = sign, which indicates that what follows is a function (formula).

- The function name, such as SUM, that indicates which operation will be performed.

- A list of arguments in parentheses, such as (A1:H1), which in this case indicates the range of cells whose values the function should use. The argument for a function is often a range of cells; you can enter an address or a range name, such as APRSALES. Some functions use more than one argument, separated by commas as in (A1,B1,H1).

You can enter functions either by just typing them into a cell or by using the Function Wizard, as you'll see later in this lesson. Table 20.1 shows Excel's most common functions that you will use most in your worksheets.

TABLE 20.1   EXCEL'S MOST COMMON FUNCTIONS

FUNCTION	EXAMPLE	DESCRIPTION
AVERAGE	=AVERAGE(B4:B9)	Calculates the mean or average of a group of numbers.
COUNT	=COUNT(A3:A7)	Counts the numeric values in a range. For example, if a range contains some cells with text and other cells with numbers, you can count how many numbers are in that range.
COUNTBLANK	=COUNTBLANK (B4:B10)	Counts all cells in a range that are blank. Cells that contain zero are not counted, nor are cells that contain "" (empty text).
IF	=IF(A3>=100, A3*2,A2*2)	Allows you to place a condition on a formula. In this example, if A3 is greater than or equal to 100, the formula A3*2 is used. If A3 is less than 100, the formula A2*2 is used instead.
MAX	=MAX(B4:B10)	Returns the maximum value in a range of cells.
MIN	=MIN(B4:B10)	Returns the minimum value in a range of cells.
PMT	=PMT(.0825/ 12,360,180000)	Calculates the monthly payment on a 30-year loan (360 monthly payments), at 8.25% a year (.0825/12 a month), for $180,000.

PMT	=PMT (.07/12,60,10000)	Calculates the monthly deposit needed to accumulate $10,000 at an annual rate of 7 per-cent (.07/12 a month), over five years (60 months).
SUM	=SUM(A1:A10)	Calculates the total in a range of cells.
SUMIF	=SUMIF(B2:B4, >100,A2:A4)	Calculates the total of the range for each cor-responding cell in sum range that matches speci-fied criteria. This example adds the cells in the range A2:A4 whose correspond-ing cell in column B is greater than 100.

Enter Text Right   When entering text into a formula, be sure to surround it with quotation marks, as in "Seattle." For example, if you wanted to total cells in column C that are next to a cell that contains the word, "Indiana", you might use this formula:

=SUMIF(B3:B10,"Indiana",C3:C10)

USING AUTOSUM

Because SUM is one of the most commonly used functions, Excel pro-vides a fast way to enter it—you click the AutoSum button in the Standard toolbar. Based on the currently selected cell, AutoSum guesses which cells you want summed. If AutoSum selects an incorrect range of cells, you can change the selection.

To use AutoSum, follow these steps:

1. Select the cell in which you want the sum inserted. Try to choose a cell at the end of a row or column of data; doing so will help AutoSum guess which cells you want added together.

2. Click the AutoSum button in the Standard toolbar. AutoSum inserts =SUM and the range address of the cells to the left of or above the selected cell (see Figure 20.1).

3. If the range Excel selected is incorrect, drag over the range you want to use, or click in the Formula bar and edit the formula.

4. Click the Enter button in the Formula bar or press Enter. Excel calculates the total for the selected range.

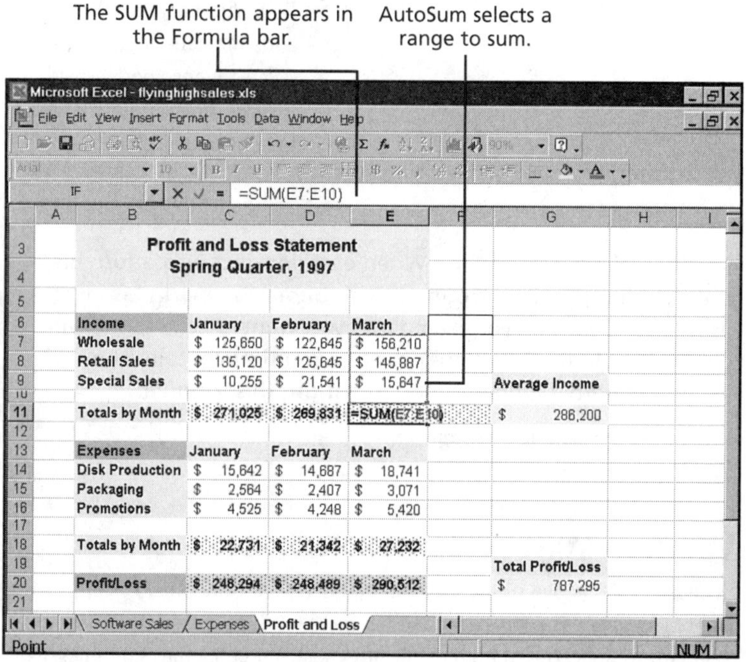

The SUM function appears in   AutoSum selects a
the Formula bar.   range to sum.

FIGURE 20.1 AutoSum inserts the SUM function and selects the cells it plans to total.

> **Quickly AutoSum**   To quickly insert the SUM function, select the cell in which you want the sum inserted and double-click the AutoSum button on the Standard toolbar. When you double-click the AutoSum button, you bypass the step where Excel displays the SUM formula and its arguments in the cell. Instead, you see the total in the cell and the SUM formula in the Formula bar. Of course, the problem with using this method is that you're not given a chance to check the range of cells AutoSum decides to add.

USING THE FUNCTION WIZARD

Although you can type a function directly into a cell just as you can type formulas, you'll find it easier to use the Function Wizard. The Function Wizard leads you through the process of inserting a function. The following steps walk you through using the Function Wizard:

1. Select the cell in which you want to insert the function. (You can insert a function by itself or as part of a formula.)

2. Type = or click the Edit Formula button on the Formula bar. The Formula Palette appears, as shown in Figure 20.2.

3. Select the function you want to insert from the Functions list by clicking the arrow on the Functions drop-down list (see Figure 20.2). If you don't see your function listed, select More Functions at the bottom of the list.

> **What's This Function?**   If you don't know a lot about a particular function and you'd like to know more, click the Help button in the Formula Palette. When the Office Assistant appears, click Help with this feature. Then click Help on selected function.

4. Enter the arguments for the formula. If you want to select a range of cells as an argument, click the Collapse Dialog button shown in Figure 20.2.

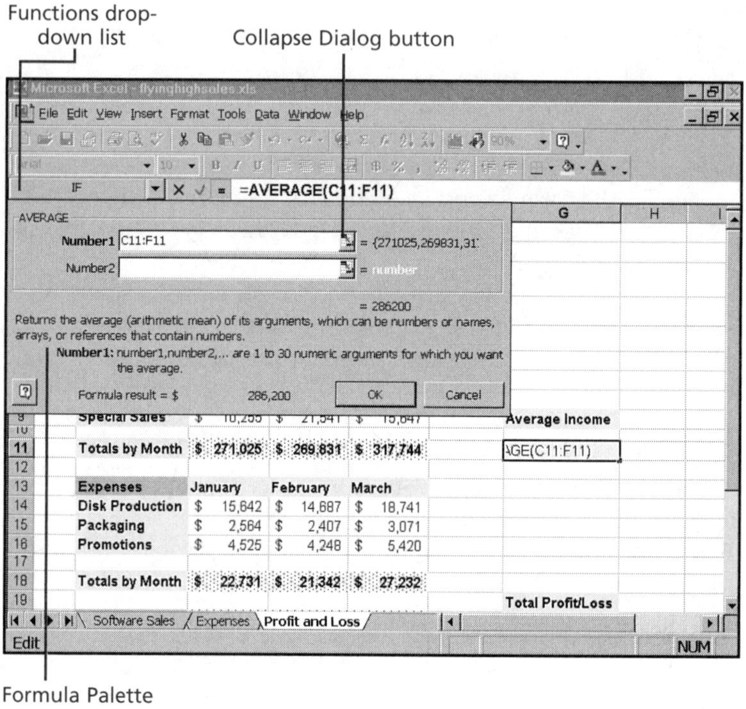

Functions drop-
down list   Collapse Dialog button

Formula Palette

FIGURE 20.2   The Function Wizard helps you enter functions.

5. After selecting a range, click the Collapse Dialog button again to
   return to the Formula Palette.

6. Click OK. Excel inserts the function and argument in the
   selected cell and displays the result.

To edit a function, click the Edit Formula button. The Formula Palette
appears. Change the arguments as needed and click OK.

In this lesson, you learned the basics of dealing with functions, and you
learned how to use Excel's Function Wizard to quickly enter functions.
You also learned how to quickly total a series of numbers with the
AutoSum tool. In the next lesson, you will learn how to format values in
your worksheet.

LESSON 21

CHANGING HOW NUMBERS LOOK

In this lesson, you will learn how to customize the appearance of numbers in your worksheet.

USING THE STYLE BUTTONS TO FORMAT NUMBERS

The Formatting toolbar (just below the Standard toolbar) contains several buttons for applying a format to your numbers, including the following:

BUTTON	NAME	EXAMPLE/DESCRIPTION
$	Currency Style	$1,200.90
%	Percent Style	20.90%
,	Comma Style	1,200.90
+.0 .00	Increase Decimal	Adds one decimal place
.00 +.0	Decrease Decimal	Deletes one decimal place

To use one of these buttons, select the cell you want to format and then click the desired button. If you want to use a format other than the ones on the Formatting toolbar, or if you'd like more control over the exact format you use, see the next section for help.

> **A Conditional Format** If you want to highlight cells that meet certain conditions by formatting only those cells (such as all values that are larger than 1,000), use conditional formatting. See Lesson 23 for more information.

FORMATTING VALUES

Numeric values are usually more than just numbers. They represent a dollar value, a date, a percent, or some other value. If the Style buttons on the Formatting toolbar do not offer the exact format you want for your numbers, don't worry. Through the Format Cells dialog box, Excel offers a wide range of number formats, listed in Table 21.1.

TABLE 21.1   EXCEL'S NUMBER FORMATS

NUMBER FORMAT	EXAMPLES	DESCRIPTION
General	10.60 $456,908.00	Excel displays your value as you enter it. In other words, this format displays currency or percent signs only if you enter them yourself.
Number	3,400.50 –120.39	The default Number format has two decimal places. Negative numbers are preceded by a minus sign, but they can also appear in red and/or parentheses.
Currency	$3,400.50 –$3,400.50	The default Currency format has two decimal places and a dollar sign. Negative numbers appear with a minus sign, but they can also appear in red and/or parentheses.
Accounting	$3,400.00 $(978.21)	Use this format to align dollar signs and decimal points in a column. The default Accounting format has two decimal places and a dollar sign.
Date	11/7	The default Date format is the month and day separated by a slash; however, you can select from numerous other formats.
Time	10:00	The default Time format is the hour and minutes separated by a colon; however, you can opt to display seconds, AM, or PM.

Percentage	99.50%	The default Percentage format has two decimal places. Excel multiplies the value in a cell by 100 and displays the result with a percent sign.
Fraction	1/2	The default Fraction format is up to one digit on either side of the slash. Use this format to display the number of digits you want on either side of the slash and the fraction type (such as halves, quarters, eighths, and so on).
Scientific	3.40E+03	The default Scientific format has two decimal places. Use this format to display numbers in scientific notation.
Text	135RV90	Use Text format to display both text and numbers in a cell as text. Excel displays the entry exactly as you type it.
Special	02110	This format is specifically designed to display ZIP codes, phone numbers, and Social Security numbers correctly, so that you don't have to enter any special characters, such as hyphens.
Custom	00.0%	Use Custom format to create your own number format. You can use any of the format codes in the Type list and then make changes to those codes. The # symbol represents a number placeholder, and 0 represents a zero placeholder.

After deciding on a suitable numeric format, follow these steps to apply it:

1. Select the cell or range that contains the values you want to format.

2. Open the Format menu and select Cells. The Format Cells dialog box appears, as shown in Figure 21.1.

3. Click the Number tab.

4. In the Category list, select the numeric format category you want to use. The sample box displays the default format for that category.

5. Make changes to the format as needed.

6. Click OK or press Enter. Excel reformats the selected cells based on your selections.

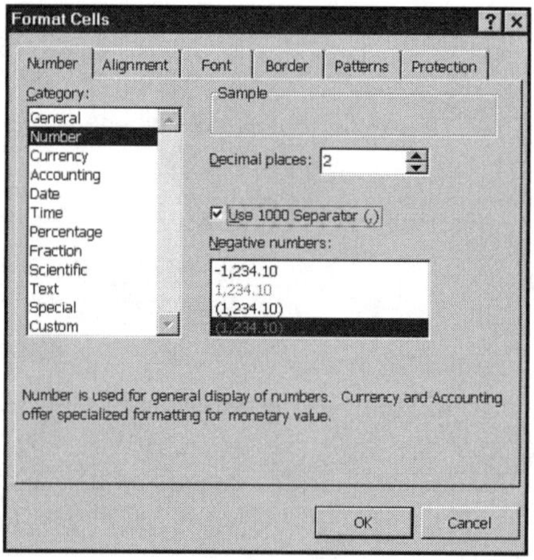

FIGURE 21.1   The Format Cells dialog box with the Number tab displayed.

You can also change the Number format of a cell by using the shortcut menu: Select the cell, right-click to display the shortcut menu, and choose Format Cells.

How Do I Get Rid of a Format?   If you want to remove a number format from a cell (and return it to General format), select the cell whose formatting you want to remove, open the Edit menu, select Clear, and select Formats.

That's Not the Date I Entered! If you enter a date in a cell that is already formatted with the Number format, the date will appear as a number. With the Number format, Excel converts the date to a value that represents the number of days between January 1, 1900 and that date. For example, 01/01/1900 equals 1, and 12/31/1900 equals 366 (1900 was a leap year). To fix your problem, change the cell's formatting from a Number format to a Date format and select a date type. (You may also need to re-enter the date, depending on whether you entered the year.)

COPYING FORMATS WITH FORMAT PAINTER

After applying a format to cell, you can easily copy that format to other cells. This works whether you're copying numeric or text formatting, or shading or borders, as you'll learn in upcoming lessons. Here's how to copy a format from one cell to another:

1. Select the cell that contains the formatting you want to copy.

2. Click the Format Painter button on the Standard toolbar. Excel copies the formatting. The mouse pointer changes into a paintbrush with a plus sign next to it.

3. Click on one cell, or drag over several cells to which you want to apply the copied formatting.

4. Release the mouse button, and Excel copies the formatting and applies it to the selected cells.

Faster Painter To paint several areas with the same formatting at one time, double-click the Format Painter button. Then drag over the first section you want to paint. The cursor remains as a paintbrush, so that you can continue to drag over other cells to paint them, too. When you're through, press Esc or click the Format Painter button again to return to a normal cursor.

In this lesson, you learned how to format numbers and to copy formatting from one cell to another. In the next lesson, you will learn how to format text.

LESSON 22

GIVING YOUR TEXT A NEW LOOK

In this lesson, you learn how to change the appearance of the text within cells.

HOW YOU CAN MAKE TEXT LOOK DIFFERENT

When you type text into a cell, Excel automatically formats it in the Arial font, which is readable, but not very fancy. You can change your text in the following ways, to improve its appearance or to set it apart from other text:

> **Font**. A typeface; for example, Arial, Courier, or Times New Roman.

> **Font Style**. For example, bold, italic, underline, or strikethrough.

Selecting the Default Font   To change the default font, open the Tools, Options dialog box and click the General tab. Make your selection in the Standard Font area. When you click the OK button, Excel makes your preference the default font.

> **Size**. For example, 10-point, 12-point, or 20-point. (The higher the point size, the bigger the text is. There are approximately 72 points in an inch.)

> **Color**. For example, Red, Magenta, or Cyan.

> **Alignment**. For example, centered, left aligned, or right aligned within the cell.

Figure 22.1 shows a worksheet after some attributes have been changed for selected text. The worksheet title is merged and centered over several cells to give it importance. The column labels use bold and underlined attributes so that they stand out against the worksheet data. The row labels, on the other hand, are more subdued, using only italic.

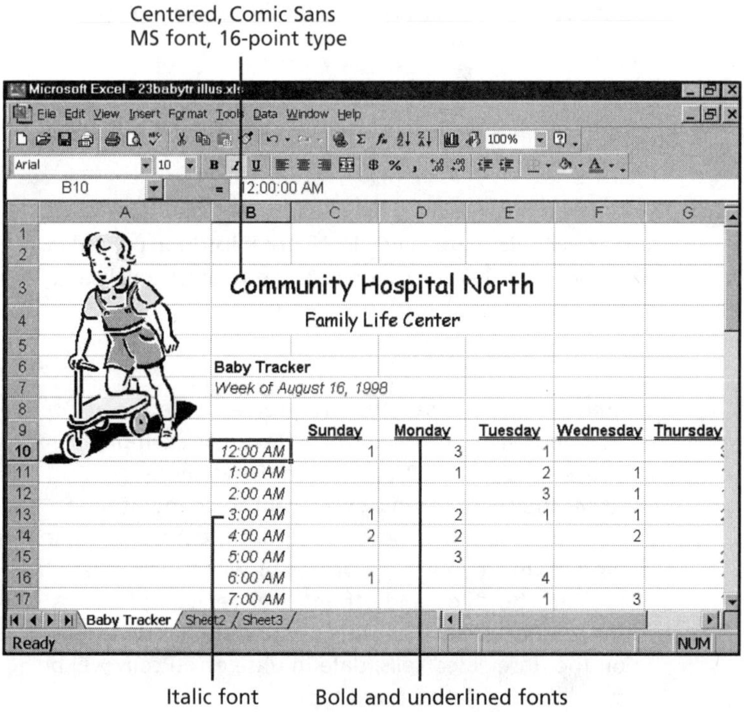

Centered, Comic Sans
MS font, 16-point type

Italic font   Bold and underlined fonts

FIGURE 22.1 A sampling of several text attributes.

CHANGING TEXT ATTRIBUTES WITH TOOLBAR BUTTONS

A faster way to enter font changes is to use the Formatting toolbar shown in Figure 22.2.

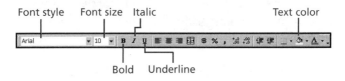

FIGURE 22.2 Use the Formatting toolbar to quickly make font changes.

To use the Formatting toolbar to change text attributes, follow these steps:

1. Select the cell or range that contains the text whose look you want to change.

2. To change the font or font size, pull down the appropriate drop-down list and click the font or size you want. You can also type the point size in the Font Size box.

3. To add an attribute (such as bold or underline), click the desired button. When selected, a button looks like it has been pressed in. You can add more than one attribute to the same text, making it bold and italic, for example.

> **Change Before You Type** You can activate the attributes you want *before* you type text. For example, if you want a title in Bold 12-point Desdemona type, select the cells for which you want to change the attributes, and then set the attributes before you start typing. Unlike in a word processor where you must turn attributes on and off, in Excel, selecting formats for cells in advance of typing your data has no effect on the unselected cells; data in unselected cells will be the default Arial 10-point type.

Font Shortcuts You can apply certain attributes quickly by using keyboard shortcuts. First select the cell, and then press Ctrl+B for bold, Ctrl+I for Italic, Ctrl+U for Single Underline (Accounting style), or Ctrl+5 for Strikethrough.

ALIGNING TEXT IN CELLS

When you enter data into a cell, that data is aligned automatically. Text is aligned on the left, and numbers are aligned on the right. Both text and numbers are initially set at the bottom of the cells. However, you can change both the vertical and the horizontal alignment of data in your cells.

Follow these steps to change the alignment:

1. Select the cell or range you want to align. If you want to center a title or other text over a range of cells, select the entire range of blank cells in which you want the text centered, including the cell that contains the text you want to center.

2. Pull down the Format menu and select Cells, or press Ctrl+1. The Format Cells dialog box appears.

3. Click the Alignment tab. The alignment options appear in front (see Figure 22.3).

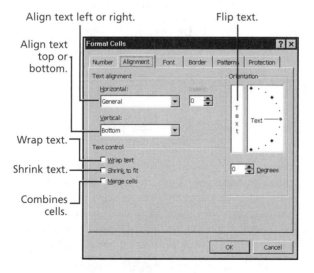

FIGURE 22.3   The Alignment options.

4. Choose from the following options to set the alignment:

Horizontal. Lets you specify a left/right alignment in the cell. (The Center Across selection centers a title or other text within a range of cells.)

Vertical. Lets you specify how you want the text aligned in relation to the top and bottom of the cells.

Orientation. Lets you flip the text sideways or print it from top to bottom (instead of left to right).

Wrap text. Tells Excel to wrap long lines of text within a cell without changing the width of the cell. (Normally, Excel displays all text in a cell on one line.)

Shrink to fit. Shrinks the text to fit within the cell's current width. If the cell's width is adjusted, the text increases or decreases in size accordingly.

Merge cells. Combines several cells into a single cell. All data is overlaid, except for the cell in the upper-left corner of the selected cells.

5. Click OK or press Enter.

A quick way to align text and numbers is to use the alignment buttons in the Formatting toolbar. The following buttons enable you to align the text:

BUTTON	NAME	DESCRIPTION
	Align Left	Places data at left edge of cell.
	Align Right	Places data at right edge of cell.
	Center	Centers data in cell.
	Merge and Center	Centers data in selected cell range.

Excel also provides you with the capability to indent your text within a cell. If you're typing a paragraph worth of information into a single cell, for example, you can indent that paragraph by selecting left alignment from the Horizontal list box in the Format Cells dialog box (as explained earlier). After selecting left alignment, set the amount of indent you want with the Indent spin box in the Format Cells dialog box.

In addition, you can add an indent quickly by clicking the following buttons on the Formatting toolbar:

BUTTON	NAME	DESCRIPTION
	Decrease Indent	Removes an indent or creates a negative indent.
	Increase Indent	Adds an indent.

CHANGING TEXT ATTRIBUTES WITH THE FORMAT CELLS DIALOG BOX

If you want to change a lot of different text attributes in one step, use the Format Cells dialog box:

1. Select the cell or range that contains the text you want to format.

2. Open the Format menu and choose Cells, or press Ctrl+1. (You can also right-click the selected cells and choose Format Cells from the shortcut menu.)

3. Click the Font tab. The Font options jump to the front, as shown in Figure 22.4.

4. Select the options you want.

5. Click OK or press Enter.

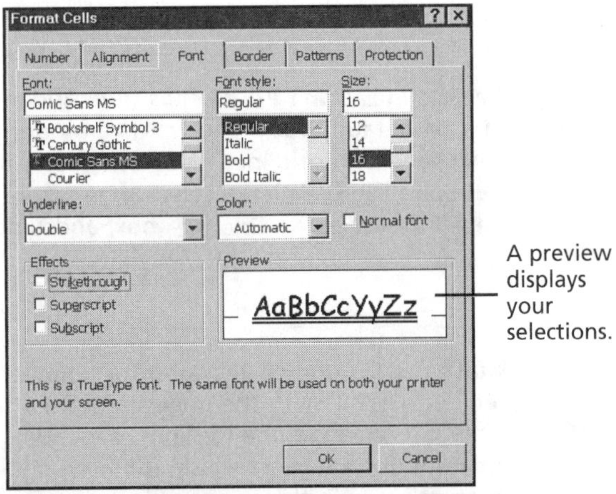

A preview displays your selections.

FIGURE 22.4   The Format Cells dialog box with the Font tab up front.

In this lesson, you learned how to customize your text formatting to achieve the look you want. In the next lesson, you will learn how to add borders and shading to the cells in your worksheet.

LESSON 23

ADDING CELL BORDERS AND SHADING

In this lesson, you will learn how to add a professional touch to your worksheets by adding borders and shading.

ADDING BORDERS TO CELLS

As you work with your worksheet onscreen, you'll notice that each cell is identified by gridlines that surround the cell. By default, these gridlines do not print; and even if you choose to print them, they appear washed out. To create well-defined lines on the printout (and onscreen, for that matter), you can add borders to selected cells or entire cell ranges. A border can appear on all four sides of a cell or only on selected sides, whichever you prefer.

 The Gridlines Don't Print? It's true, gridlines do not print by default. But if you want to try printing your worksheet with gridlines first just to see what it looks like, open the File menu, select Page Setup, click the Sheet tab, check the Gridlines box, and click OK.

What's the Difference Between Text Underlining and a Cell Border? With the underline format explained in the last lesson, a line (or lines, depending on which underline format you choose) is placed under the cell's contents—within the cell's borders. In this lesson, you'll learn how to add a line to the bottom of a cell's border, producing a different effect. Which is right? Whichever one you like best.

To add borders to a cell or range, perform the following steps:

1. Select the cell around which you want a border to appear.

2. Open the Format menu and choose Cells. The Format Cells dialog box appears.

3. Click the Border tab to see the Border options shown in Figure 23.1.

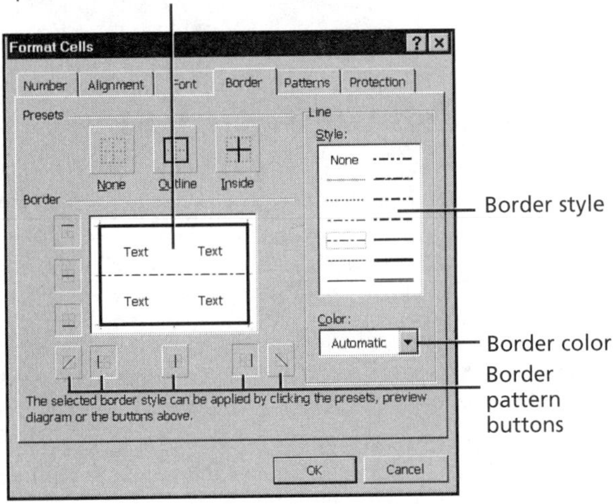

Click inside the Border box to place a border at that location.

FIGURE 23.1 Choose border options from the Format Cells dialog box.

4. Select the desired position, style (thickness), and color for the border. You can click inside the Border box itself, or you can click a preset border pattern button to add your border.

5. Click OK or press Enter.

To add borders quickly, select the cells around which you want the border to appear, and then click the arrow to the right of the Borders button in the Formatting toolbar. Click the desired border. If you click the Borders button itself (instead of the arrow), Excel automatically adds the border line you last chose to the selected cells.

> **Hiding Gridlines**   When adding borders to a work-
> sheet, you might need to hide the gridlines so when
> you look at the worksheet onscreen, you have a good
> idea of how the borders will look when printed. Open
> the Tools menu, select Options, click the View tab, and
> select Gridlines to remove the check mark from the
> check box. Selecting this option has no effect on
> whether the gridlines actually print, only on whether
> they are displayed onscreen. (If you want gridlines to
> print, apply cell borders to selected cells, or use the
> Page Setup dialog box, as described in Lesson 17.)

Adding Shading to Cells

For a simple but dramatic effect, add shading to your worksheets. With
shading, you can add a color or gray shading to the background of a cell.
You can add shading at full strength or at partial strength by selecting a
pattern, such as a diagonal. Figure 23.2 illustrates some of the effects you
can create with shading.

Follow these steps to add shading to a cell or range. As you make your
selections, keep in mind that if you plan to print your worksheet with a
black-and-white printer, your pretty colors may not be different enough to
create the effect you want. Select colors that contrast well in value (inten-
sity), and use the Print Preview command (as explained in Lesson 16) to
view your results in black and white before you print.

1. Select the cell you want to shade.

2. Open the Format menu and choose Cells.

3. Click the Patterns tab. Excel displays the shading options (see
    Figure 23.3).

4. Click the Pattern drop-down arrow, and you will see a grid that
    contains all the colors from the color palette, as well as patterns.
    Select the shading color and pattern you want to use. The Color
    options let you choose a color for the overall shading. The
    Pattern options let you select a black or colored pattern that is
    placed on top of the cell shading color (the background color)
    you selected. A preview of the result appears in the Sample box,
    but keep in mind that the result will vary if you are using a
    black-and-white printer.

5. When you like the results you see, click OK or press Enter.

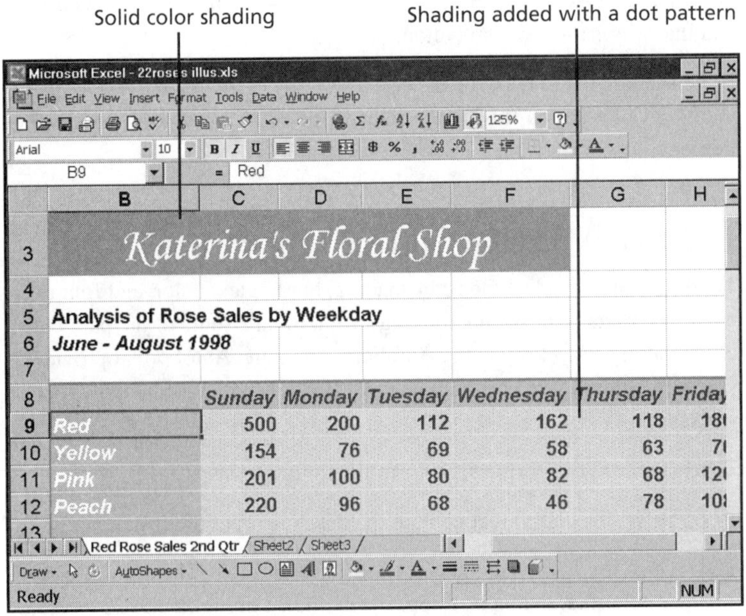

Solid color shading   Shading added with a dot pattern

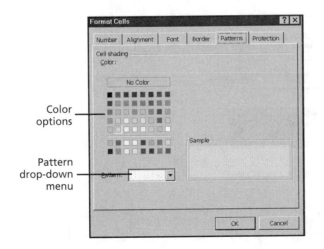

FIGURE 23.2   A worksheet with added shading.

FIGURE 23.3   The Patterns tab of the Format Cells dialog box.

A quick way to add cell shading (without a pattern) is to select the cells you want to shade, click the arrow to the right of the Fill Color button, and click the color you want to use. If you click the button itself, you'll add the color shown on the button.

 If the shading is too dark for the cell data to be easily read, consider using the Font Color button (just to the right of the Fill Color button) to select a lighter color for the text.

Using AutoFormat

Tired of trying to select the right shading, border, text color, and font to make your data professional looking? Well, to take some of the pain out of formatting, Excel offers the AutoFormat feature. AutoFormat provides you with a number of predesigned table formats that you can apply to a worksheet.

To use predesigned formats, perform the following steps:

1. Select the cell(s) that contain the data you want to format.

2. Open the Format menu and choose AutoFormat. The AutoFormat dialog box appears, as shown in Figure 23.4.

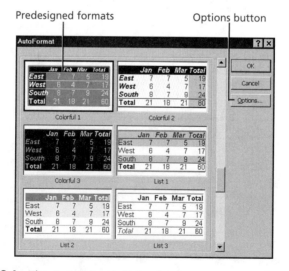

Figure 23.4   The AutoFormat dialog box.

3. Scroll through the list and click the predesigned format you want to use.

4. To exclude certain elements from an AutoFormat, click the Options button and choose the formats you want to turn off.

5. Click OK, and Excel formats your table to make it look like the one in the preview area.

Easier to Use If you're upgrading from an older version of Excel, you'll find AutoFormat even easier to use, with large pictures that show you what each format really looks like.

Yech! I Chose That? If you don't like what AutoFormat did to your worksheet, click the Undo button.

APPLYING CONDITIONAL FORMATTING

If you want to highlight particular values in your worksheet, you can use conditional formatting. For example, if you want to highlight all sales figures under a particular value, you could apply a conditional red shading.

To apply conditional formatting, follow these steps:

1. Select the first cell to which you want to apply conditional formatting. (Select only one cell; after you're done, you can copy the formatting to additional cells.)

2. Open the Format menu and select Conditional Formatting. The Conditional Formatting dialog box appears, as shown in Figure 23.5.

3. To apply a format based on the value found in a selected cell, choose Cell value is from the Condition 1 list.

   To apply a format based on the result of a formula that involves cells outside the range of cells to which you want to apply the conditioning, select Formula is from the Condition 1 list.

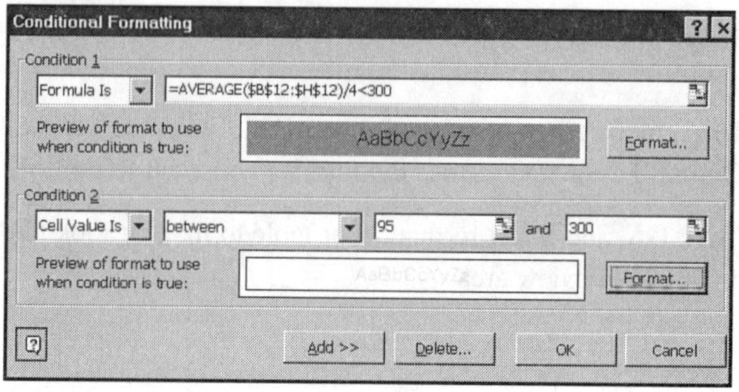

FIGURE 23.5   Apply formats conditionally to highlight certain values.

4. In the Condition 1 text box, enter the value or formula you want to use as the condition that determines when Excel can apply the formatting you select.

If you selected Cell value is in step 3, you can still enter a formula in the text box, but the formula must result in a value. For example, you could enter:

Cell value is   greater than   =C22*.25

If you choose Formula is in step 3, the formula you enter must result in a true or false value. For example, if you wanted to format some cells based on whether or not a corresponding value in column A is less than 20% of projected sales (cell D12), you could use this formula:

Formula is   =A1<20%*$D$12

5. Click the Format button and select the format you want to apply when the conditions are met. Click OK to return to the Conditional Formatting dialog box.

6. You can add more conditions by clicking Add and repeating steps 3 to 5.

7. When you finish adding conditions, click OK.

8. After applying the conditional formatting to the first cell, click the Format Painter button, and then drag over any additional cells to which you want to copy the conditional formatting.

In this lesson, you learned some ways to enhance the appearance of your worksheets. In the next lesson, you will learn how to create charts from your worksheet data.

LESSON 24

CREATING
CHARTS

In this lesson, you will learn to create graphical representations (charts) of workbook data.

CHARTING TERMINOLOGY

Before you start creating charts, you should familiarize yourself with the following terminology:

> **Data Series**. The bars, pie wedges, lines, or other elements that represent plotted values in a chart. For example, a chart might show a set of similar bars that reflects a series of values for the same item. The bars in the same data series would all have the same pattern. If you have more than one pattern of bars, each pattern would represent a separate data series. For instance, charting the sales for Territory 1 versus Territory 2 would require two data series—one for each territory. Often, data series correspond to rows of data in your worksheet.

> **Categories**. Categories reflect the number of elements in a series. You might have two data series that compare the sales of two different territories and four categories that compare these sales over four quarters. Some charts have only one category, and others have several. Categories normally correspond to the columns in your worksheet, with the category labels coming from the column headings.

> **Axis**. One side of a chart. A two-dimensional chart has an x-axis (horizontal) and a y-axis (vertical). The x-axis contains the data series and categories in the chart. If you have more than one category, the x-axis often contains labels that define what each category represents. The y-axis reflects the values of the bars, lines, or plot

points. In a three-dimensional chart, the z-axis represents the vertical plane, and the x-axis (distance) and y-axis (width) represent the two sides on the floor of the chart.

Legend. Defines the separate series of a chart. For example, the legend for a pie chart will show what each piece of the pie represents.

Gridlines. Typically, gridlines appear along the value or y-axis, although they can emanate from the x-axis as well. Gridlines help you determine a point's exact value.

CHART TYPES

With Excel, you can create many different types of charts. Some common chart types are shown in Figure 24.1. The chart type you choose depends on what kind of data you're trying to chart, and on how you want to present that data. These are the major chart types and their purposes:

Pie. Use this chart type to show the relationship among parts of a whole.

Bar. Use this chart type to compare values at a given point in time.

Column. Similar to the bar chart; use this chart type to emphasize the difference between items.

Line. Use this chart type to emphasize trends and the change of values over time.

Scatter. Similar to a line chart; use this chart type to emphasize the difference between two sets of values.

Area. Similar to the line chart; use this chart type to emphasize the amount of change in values over time.

Most of these basic chart types also come in three-dimensional varieties. In addition to looking more professional than the standard flat charts, 3D charts can often help your audience distinguish between different sets of data.

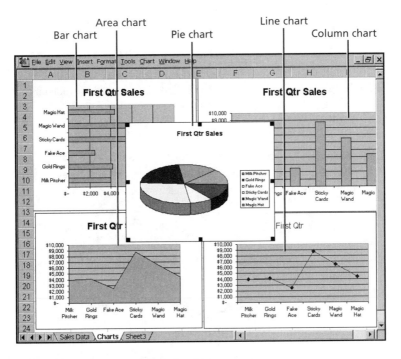

FIGURE 24.1   Common Excel chart types.

CREATING A CHART

You can place your new chart on the same worksheet that contains the chart data (an embedded chart) or on a separate worksheet (a chart sheet). If you create an embedded chart, it is typically printed side-by-side with your worksheet data. If you create a chart on a separate worksheet, you can print it independently. Both types of charts are linked to the worksheet data that they represent, so when you change the data, the chart is automatically updated.

> **Embedded Charts**   A chart that is placed on the same worksheet as the data used to create the chart is called *embedded*. A chart can also be placed on a chart sheet in the workbook so that the worksheet and chart are separate. Embedded charts are useful for showing the actual data and its graphic representation side-by-side. On the other hand, when a chart is placed on its own sheet, it's easier to locate and print.

The Chart Wizard button on Standard toolbar enables you to quickly create a chart. To use the Chart Wizard, follow these steps:

1. Select the data you want to chart. If you typed column or row labels (such as Qtr 1, Qtr 2, and so on) that you want included in the chart, make sure you select them, too.

2. Click the Chart Wizard button on the Standard toolbar.

3. The Chart Wizard Step 1 of 4 dialog box appears, as shown in Figure 24.2. Select a Chart type and a Chart sub-type (a variation on the selected chart type). Click Next>.

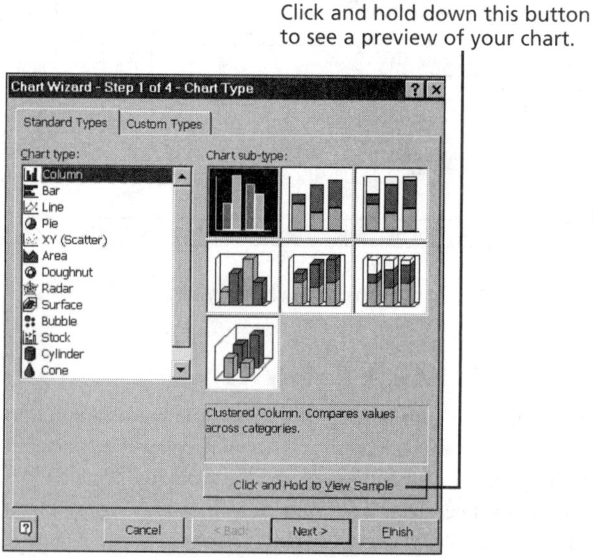

Click and hold down this button
to see a preview of your chart.

FIGURE 24.2   Chart Wizard asks you to choose the chart type.

4. Next you're asked if the selected range is correct. You can correct the range by typing a new range or by clicking the Collapse Dialog button (located at the right end of the Data range text box) and selecting the range you want to use.

5. By default, Excel assumes that your different data series are stored in rows. You can change this to columns if necessary by clicking the Series in Columns option. When you're through, click Next>.

6. Click the various tabs to change options for your chart (see Figure 24.3). For example, you can delete the legend by clicking the Legend tab and deselecting Show Legend. You can add a chart title on the Titles tab. Add data labels (labels which display the actual value being represented by each bar, line, and so on) by clicking the Data Labels tab. When you finish making changes, click Next>.

Click a tab and select the options you want.

A preview of your chart appears here.

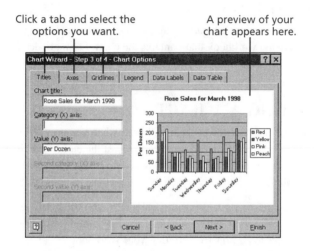

FIGURE 24.3   Select from various chart appearance options.

7. Finally, you're asked if you want to embed the chart (as an object) in the current worksheet (or any other existing worksheet in the workbook), or if you want to create a new worksheet for it. Make your selection and click the Finish button. Your completed chart appears.

Moving and Resizing a Chart   To move an embedded chart, click anywhere in the chart area and drag it to the new location. To change the size of a chart, select the chart, and then drag one of its handles (the black squares that border the chart). Drag a corner handle to change the height and width, or drag a side handle to change only one dimension. (Note that you can't really resize a chart that is on a sheet by itself.)

> **Create a Chart Fast!** To create a chart quickly, select the data you want to use and press F11. Excel creates a column chart (the default chart type) on its own sheet. You can then customize the chart as needed.

SAVING CHARTS

The charts you create are part of the current workbook. To save a chart, simply save the workbook that contains the chart. For more details, refer to Lesson 3, "Saving and Closing Workbook Files."

PRINTING A CHART

If a chart is an embedded chart, it will print when you print the worksheet that contains the chart. If you want to print just the embedded chart, click it to select it, and then open the File menu and select Print. Make sure that the Selected Chart option is turned on. Then click OK to print the chart.

If you created a chart on a separate worksheet, you can print the chart separately by printing only that worksheet. For more information about printing, refer to Lesson 16, "Printing Your Workbook."

In this lesson, you learned about the different chart types and how to create them. You also learned how to save and print charts. In the next lesson, you will learn how to enhance your charts.

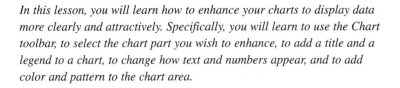

LESSON 25

ENHANCING YOUR CHARTS

In this lesson, you will learn how to enhance your charts to display data more clearly and attractively. Specifically, you will learn to use the Chart toolbar, to select the chart part you wish to enhance, to add a title and a legend to a chart, to change how text and numbers appear, and to add color and pattern to the chart area.

SELECTING A CHART PART

A chart is made up of several objects. For example, a chart may have a title, a legend, and various data series. To enhance these elements of your chart, you must first select the part of the chart you want to change. To do this, click that part or select it from the Chart Objects box on the Chart toolbar (see the next section for help with the toolbar). When a part is selected, handles (tiny black squares) form a box around it, as shown in Figure 25.1.

When a part is selected, you can move it by dragging it wherever you want: click on the object, hold down the mouse button and drag the object, then release the mouse button to "drop" it. To resize a part, select it and then drag one of its handles outward to make the object larger or inward to make it smaller. When the object is the size you want it, release the mouse button. You can resize the whole chart by selecting it first and then dragging one of its handles.

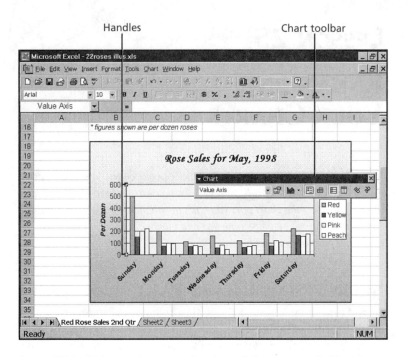

FIGURE 25.1   When a chart part is selected, it's surrounded by handles.

THE CHART TOOLBAR

You can use the Chart toolbar to change how your chart looks. Normally, the Chart toolbar is displayed whenever you select a chart element, but if not, you can turn it on by opening the View menu, selecting Toolbars, and then selecting Chart.

Table 25.1 shows each button on the Chart toolbar, and explains its purpose.

TABLE 25.1   BUTTONS ON THE CHART TOOLBAR

BUTTON	NAME	USE
Value Axis ▾	Chart Objects	Click here to select the part of the chart you want to change. Or, you can click the part itself.

	Format Object	Click here to change the formatting of the object whose name appears in the Chart Objects text box.
	Chart Type	Click the arrow to select another chart type; line instead of bar, for example. If you click the button itself, the displayed chart type will be applied.
	Legend	Click this to display or hide the legend.
	Data Table	Click here to add a data table (a grid which displays the data from which the chart was created).
	By Row	Click here if your data series are stored in rows.
	By Column	Click here if your data series are stored in columns.
	Angle Text Downward	Click here to angle text in selected area downward.
	Angle Text Upward	Click here to angle text in selected area upward.

CHANGING THE CHART TYPE

To change the type of chart from a line chart to a pie chart, for example, follow these steps:

1. Click the chart to select it, or choose Chart Area from the Chart Objects drop-down list on the Chart toolbar. Handles appear around the whole chart.

2. Click the Chart Type button to change the chart to the displayed type, or click the drop-down arrow and select another type.

The Chart I Want Isn't Displayed!   To change to a chart type that is not on the list, open the Chart menu and select Chart Type. You can choose from a number of chart types in this dialog box.

ADDING A TITLE AND A LEGEND

You can add various titles to a chart to help indicate what the chart is all about. You can add a chart title that appears at the top of the chart, and you can add axis titles that appear along the x- and y-axes (and the z-axis as well, if the chart is a 3D chart). You can also add a legend—a small table that describes what each element in the chart represents.

Here's how you do it:

1. Click the chart to select it, or choose Chart Area from the Chart Objects drop-down list on the Chart toolbar. Handles appear around the whole chart.

2. Open the Chart menu and select Chart Options. The Chart Options dialog box appears, as shown in Figure 25.2.

Enter your title here.   Axis labels

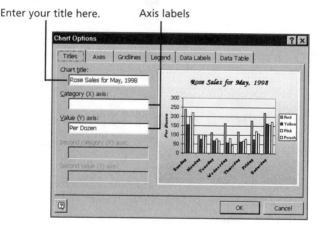

FIGURE 25.2   Add additional titles to your chart.

3. Click the Titles tab, and then add the titles you want. A sample chart appears on the right so you can see what your changes will look like.

4. To add a legend, click the Legend tab. Click the Show legend option if needed to turn it on. Then select where you want the legend placed.

5. When you finish, click OK.

> **More Text** If you want to add text that is not a chart title or axis title, click the Drawing button on the Standard toolbar to display the Drawing toolbar. Click the Text Box button, and then drag the mouse pointer to create the text box. When you release the mouse button, an insertion point appears inside the text box. Type your text. You also can use this technique to add text to your worksheets.

FORMATTING TEXT AND NUMBERS ON A CHART

All the text on a chart appears inside its own text box. To format text or numbers on a chart, follow these steps:

1. Click the text or numbers you want to change, or select it from the Chart Objects drop-down list on the Chart toolbar.

2. Click the Format Object button on the Chart toolbar. The dialog box that appears differs slightly from object to object, but no matter.

3. Click the Font tab. The Font options enable you to change the font, style, size, and color of the text (see Figure 25.3).

4. To change the text's alignment, click the Alignment tab. Here you can choose to display the text at an angle to save room, if necessary.

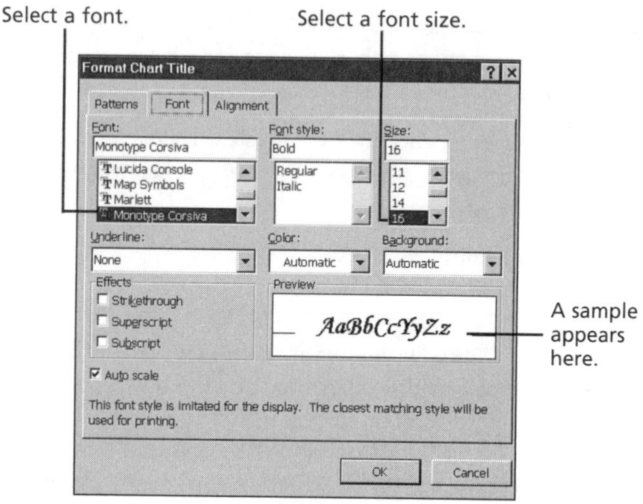

Select a font.   Select a font size.

FIGURE 25.3   Change the look of text with options on the Font tab.

5. To change the way numbers look, click the Number tab. Then select a category and choose from the other available options, as shown in Figure 25.4.

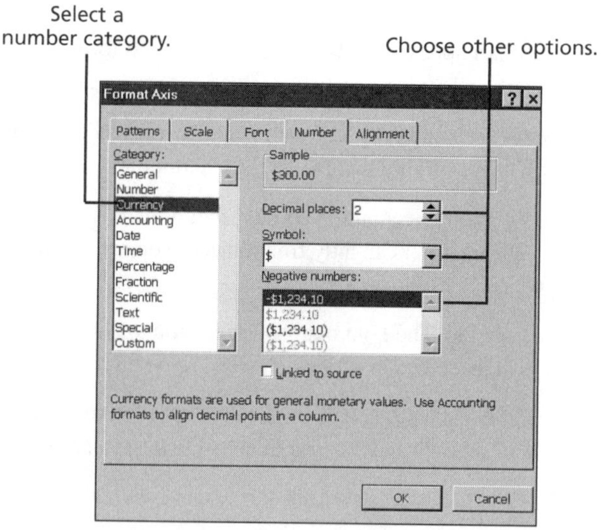

Select a
number category.
Choose other options.

FIGURE 25.4   Change the look of numbers on the Number tab.

6. Click OK when you are finished.

ENHANCING THE CHART AREA

One way to make your chart stand out is to change its frame. The frame is the box in which the chart appears. You can also change the background that fills this frame. In addition, you can enhance the plot area, the area in which the data appears, by adding a colorful border or changing its color or pattern.

To enhance the chart or plot area, follow these steps:

1. Click the object you want to change, or select it from the Chart Objects drop-down list on the Chart toolbar. To change the chart's background or border, select Chart Area. To change the plot background or border, select Plot Area instead.

2. Click the Format Object button on the Chart toolbar.

3. Click the Patterns tab, and you'll see the options shown in Figure 25.5.

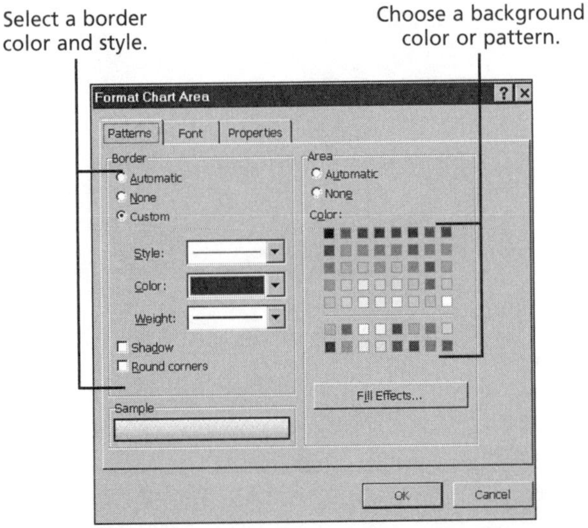

Select a border color and style.

Choose a background color or pattern.

FIGURE **25.5** Change the background and border of your chart with the Patterns tab.

4. To change the border of the selected area, choose from the options in the Border section. You can change the style, color, and weight (thickness) of the border. Your selections appear in the Sample area so you can see how they'll look.

5. To change the background of the selected area, choose from the options in the Area section. Here, you can select a color for the background. If you click Fill Effects, you can choose from various gradient fills, textures, and patterns. You can even use a graphic as the background for your chart if you want.

6. When you're through, click OK.

In this lesson, you learned how to improve the appearance of your chart. In the next lesson, you will learn other ways in which you can customize your chart.

LESSON 26

MORE WAYS TO ENHANCE CHARTS

In this lesson, you will learn additional ways in which you can customize your charts. Specifically, you will learn how to modify the gridline display, adjust the perspective of 3D charts, customize the value axis, and add more data to a chart.

DISPLAYING OR HIDING GRIDLINES

By default, horizontal gridlines appear in most Excel charts (except certain types of charts, such as pie charts). You can change to vertical gridlines only or use both a combination of horizontal and vertical. In addition, you can change the value represented by the gridline's upper and lower limits and the interval between gridlines. Also, you can display minor gridlines.

> **Major and Minor Gridlines** *Major gridlines* help you pinpoint exact locations in a chart without cluttering the chart. When major gridlines don't provide enough detail, you can use minor gridlines as well. *Minor gridlines* fall between the major intervals on the axis.

To change to vertical gridlines (or to both horizontal and vertical gridlines) or to display minor gridlines, this is what you do:

1. Click the chart. Then open the Chart menu and select Chart Options. The Chart Options dialog box appears.

2. Click the Gridlines tab.

3. Select the gridlines you want to display. Your selections appear in the sample area so you can see how they'll look.

4. Click OK.

CHANGING THE START AND STOP VALUES OF THE VALUE AXIS

You can change the start and stop value used on the value axis (the axis against which the values are plotted—typically, the y-axis), and you can change the interval between gridlines. You might need to do this, for example, to shorten the value axis to draw attention to the difference between two data series. Follow these steps:

1. Select Value Axis from the Chart Objects drop-down list on the Chart toolbar.

2. Click the Format Object button.

3. Click the Scale tab, and you'll see the options shown in Figure 26.1.

4. Change the Minimum or Maximum values used to plot the data if you want. For example, if the maximum value shown on the Scale tab is 12,000, but the maximum data value is only 9,800, you might want to change the maximum value to 10,000 to tighten up the plot area.

5. To change the interval between gridlines, adjust the value under Major unit. If you're displaying minor gridlines too, you may want to adjust that Minor unit value as well.

> **Large Numbers?**   If your worksheet uses large numbers, such as 12,000,000, you can now abbreviate them to just 12, and display a label along the Value axis instead, such as "Millions."

Format Axis

Patterns | **Scale** | Font | Number | Alignment

Value (Y) axis scale

Auto

☑ Mi̱nimum: 0

☑ Ma̱ximum: 300

☑ Ma̱jor unit: 50

☑ Mi̱nor unit: 10

☑ Category (X) axis

Crosses at: 0

Display u̱nits: None ▼   ☑ Show display units label on chart

☐ Lo̱garithmic scale
☐ Values in ṟeverse order
☐ Category (X) axis crosses at ma̱ximum value

OK   Cancel

FIGURE 26.1   Change the gridline values with the Scale tab.

6. You can adjust the point at which the x-axis crosses the y-axis by changing the value under Category (X) axis crosses at. If you want the x-axis to cross the y-axis at its highest value (you want to display the categories at the top of the chart), select the Category (X) axis crosses at maximum value option instead.

7. If the values you are plotting are large, you can reduce the scale used on the Value axis by selecting an option from the Display units drop-down list. For example, if you select Billions, then values on the Value axis such as 6,000,000,000 are displayed as simply "6."

8. To recalculate the minimum, maximum, and interval values based on the range of data values in your chart, select the Logarithmic scale option.

Negative Idea   If your chart contains negative values, do not select the Logarithmic Scale option.

9. To change the order in which values are displayed along the value axis, select the Values in reverse order option.

10. When you're finished, click OK.

CHANGING THE CATEGORY AXIS

You can customize the category axis (the x-axis) as well. For example, you can increase the space between columns (or bars, and so on). To learn how, follow these steps:

1. Choose Category Axis from the Chart Objects drop-down list on the Chart toolbar.

2. Click the Format Object button.

3. Click the Scale tab, and you'll see the options shown in Figure 26.2.

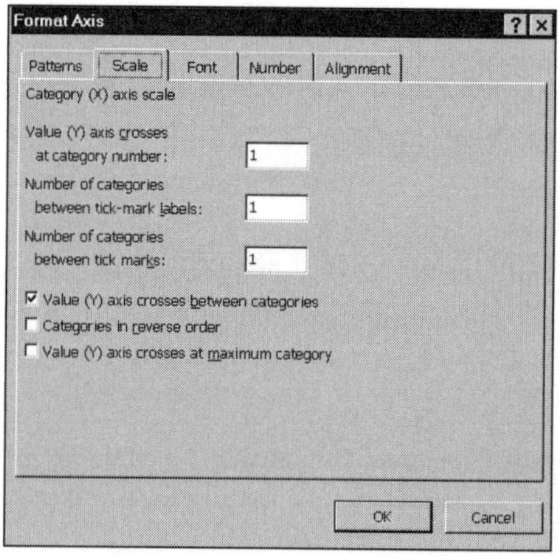

FIGURE 26.2   You can change the Category display, as well.

4. On most charts, you can change the point at which the value axis (y-axis) crosses the category axis (x-axis) by entering a different category number in the Value axis crosses at category number box.

5. To display a label under every other category, enter a 2 in the Number of categories between tick-mark labels text box. To label every third category instead, enter a 3, and so on.

6. To display more categories between the tick-marks on the x-axis, change the value under Number of categories between tick-marks.

7. If the Value (Y) axis crosses between categories option is not selected, then no space will appear between the first and last categories and the edges of the plot area.

8. Reverse the order in which the categories are plotted by selecting the Categories in reverse order option.

9. If you want the value labels to appear on the right-hand side of the plot area instead of the left, select the Value (Y) axis crosses at maximum category option.

10. Click OK when you're through.

CHANGING THE PERSPECTIVE OF 3D CHARTS

3D charts are commonly used to illustrate volume. In order to make the various three-dimensional elements stand out, you may want to tilt the plot area or rotate it. Here's how you do that:

1. Choose Corners from the Chart Objects drop-down list on the Chart toolbar.

2. Click the lower-right corner, as shown in Figure 26.3.

3. Drag a corner to change the 3D perspective of the plot area. A wire frame follows the mouse pointer to show you approximately how your chart will look in that perspective.

4. When you like the perspective, release the mouse button. Excel redraws your 3D chart to match the perspective you have chosen.

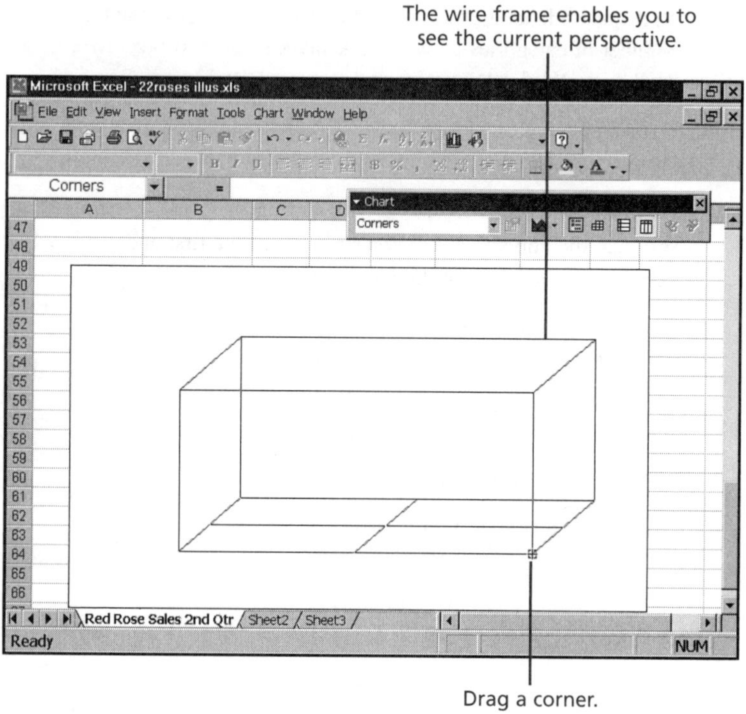

The wire frame enables you to
see the current perspective.

Drag a corner.

FIGURE 26.3   Changing the 3D perspective.

SELECTING DATA SERIES OPTIONS

Each chart type comes with special options that you can select to emphasize certain values in your particular chart. For example, a column chart
allows you to set the gap width (the width between categories) and the
overlap (the amount that columns in different series overlap). In addition,
if the column chart uses only a single series, by default all the columns
are the same color. You can tell Excel to display them in different colors if
you like.

On a line chart, you can add drop lines (lines that help you view the dif-
ferences between different series), change the markers, and add high-low
lines. Each chart type has its own special options from which you can
choose.

To select from the various data series options, follow these steps:

1. Choose Series "x" from the Chart Objects drop-down list on the Chart toolbar.

 Which Series? If your chart includes several series, select the series you want to change. However, most of the time, it doesn't matter which series you select, because the majority of these options apply to all the series in a chart, and not to a particular one.

2. Click the Format Object button. The Format Data Series dialog box appears.

3. Click the Options tab.

4. Select from the available options. For example, on a column chart, adjust the gap width if you like.

5. Click the Patterns tab. In addition to being able to change the color choices of the selected series, additional options sometimes appear here. For example, on a line chart, you can change the style of the marker from this tab. Select whatever options you want.

6. Click OK when you're through.

CHANGING DATA SERIES VALUES

As you fine-tune your chart, you may discover that you originally selected the wrong cells for a particular data series. Or you may want to add an additional series to a chart. Both options are easy to complete using the Source Data dialog box. Here's how:

1. Click the chart to select it.

2. Open the Chart menu and select Source Data. The Source Data dialog box opens, as shown in Figure 26.4.

3. Click the Series tab.

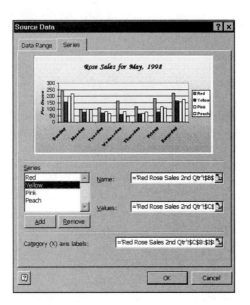

FIGURE 26.4   Change your data series.

4. To remove a series, select it from the Series list and click Remove.

5. To add a new series, click Add. Then either type the appropriate range address in the Name and Values text boxes, or click the Collapse Dialog button and select the ranges you want to use from the worksheet.

6. Repeat step 5 to add additional series. The sample chart changes to reflect your additions and deletions.

7. When you finish making changes to your data series, click OK.

In this lesson, you learned additional ways you can customize your chart. In the next lesson, you will learn how to save and publish your Excel creations to the Internet.

LESSON 27

SAVING AND PUBLISHING WORKBOOKS TO THE INTERNET

In this lesson, you will learn how to prepare worksheets for use on the Internet.

SAVING A WORKBOOK TO AN FTP SITE

An FTP site is a special computer attached to the Internet (or intranet) that handles only file transfers (file uploads and downloads). You can save your workbook to an FTP site on the Internet (or a local intranet), provided you have the permission to do so:

1. First, add the FTP site to the Save As dialog box by opening the Save in list and selecting Add/Modify FTP Locations. The Add/Modify FTP dialog box appears, as shown in Figure 27.1.

2. In the Name of FTP site: text box, enter the site's address, such as **ftp.microsoft.com**.

3. Select Log on as, either Anonymous or User, and enter a password if necessary.

4. Click OK.

5. After the site has been added to the Save As dialog box, you can select it from the FTP Locations folder in the Save in list.

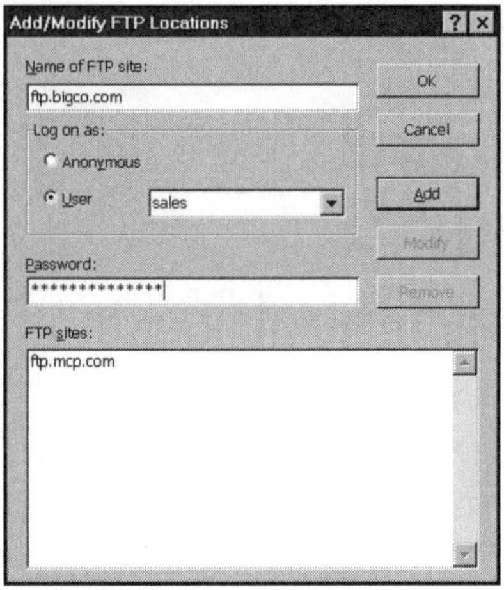

FIGURE 27.1   Adding a new FTP site.

SAVING A WORKBOOK IN HTML FORMAT

You can save your Excel data to a Web site (or on your company's intranet) by converting your workbook to HTML format. When you save a workbook (or part of a workbook) in this way, it can be viewed through a Web browser.

> **HTML**   Short for *HyperText Markup Language*, HTML is the language in which data is presented on the World Wide Web. To display your Excel data on the Web, you must convert it to this format.

If you publish an entire workbook, then it can be viewed but it cannot be changed: The data is considered *static*. However, you can update the data yourself as needed by saving the workbook again. You can also publish part of a workbook, such as a worksheet, as static data.

If you want to make your data *interactive* so that a user can view it and change it, you must publish only part of your workbook at a time. You can publish a worksheet, a chart, a PivotTable, or a selected range, to name a few.

It's New to You!   If you tried to use the HTML publishing feature in Excel 97 and gave up because it was too complex, now's the time to give it another try. In Excel 2000, the process is almost as simple as saving a workbook, as you'll soon see.

PUBLISHING STATIC DATA

To publish data that cannot be changed, follow these steps:

1. If you're not publishing the entire workbook, select the item that you want to publish.

2. Open the File menu and select Save as Web Page. The Save As dialog box appears, as shown in Figure 27.2.

Choose a location for the HTML file.   Select what you want to publish.

Save As	? x
Save in: ☐ My Web Folder	▼ ⇦ 🗈 ⬕ ⬕ ⬕ ⬕ ▾ Tools ▾

History
My Documents
Desktop
Favorites
Web Folders

Save: ○ Entire Workbook   ○ Selection: TotalExpensesFe   Publish...
        ☐ Add interactivity

Page title: Change Title...
File name: flyinghighsales.htm   🖫 Save
Save as type: Web Page (*.htm; *.html)   Cancel

Type a name for the file.

FIGURE 27.2   The Save As dialog box.

3. In the Save in list, type (or select) the Internet or intranet location on which you want to save the workbook. You can also save the HTML file to a local hard drive.

> **Hey, Look Me Over!**   Prior to publishing your data,
> you may want to save it to a local hard drive first. You
> can then view it in your Web browser and, using an
> HTML editor, make any changes to it as needed. You
> can then publish the HTML file to its permanent loca-
> tion on your company's intranet or the Internet.

4. Type a name for the HTML file in the File name text box.

5. If you want, click Change Title and then change the title for the
Web page (the HTML file). (The title appears in the title bar of
the users' Web browsers when they are viewing your page.)

6. Perform either of the following:

To save the entire workbook, select Entire Workbook, then click
Save. (Skip the remaining steps.)

To save a part of the workbook (such as a worksheet or a chart),
choose Selection and click Publish. The Publish as Web Page dialog
box appears, as shown in Figure 27.3.

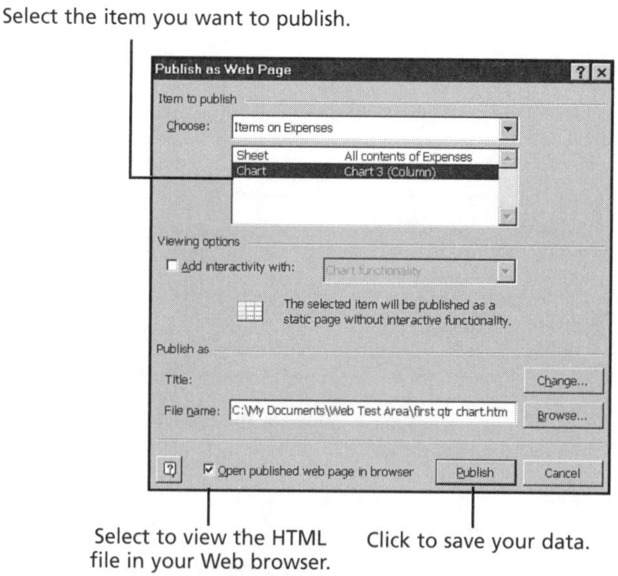

Select the item you want to publish.

Select to view the HTML   Click to save your data.
file in your Web browser.

FIGURE 27.3   The Publish as Web Page dialog box.

7. Select the item you want to publish from the Choose list.

8. If you want, select Open published web page in browser to launch your Web browser so you can view the HTML file.

9. Click Publish.

PUBLISHING INTERACTIVE DATA

When you save part of a workbook, such as a worksheet or a chart, in interactive format, users can both view and make changes to it. You might want to use this option if you're publishing group data to your company's intranet.

To publish interactive data:

1. Select the item that you want to publish.

2. Open the File menu and select Save as Web Page. The Save As dialog box appears. (See Figure 27.2.)

3. In the Save in list, type (or select) the Internet or intranet location on which you want to save the workbook. You can also save the HTML file to a local hard drive.

4. Type a name for the HTML file in the File name text box.

5. If you want, click Change Title and then change the title for the Web page (the HTML file). (The title appears in the title bar of the users' Web browsers when they are viewing your page.)

6. Click Publish. The Publish as Web Page dialog box appears, as shown in Figure 27.4.

7. Select the item you want to publish from the Choose list.

8. Choose the Add interactivity with option, then select the type of interactivity you desire:

> **Spreadsheet functionality.** Allows users to enter, update, copy, move, delete, format, sort, or filter data.

> **PivotTable functionality.** Allows users to change the layout of a PivotTable's data, or to sort, filter, or change the data.

> **Chart functionality.** Allows users to change the source data for a chart, which then updates the chart itself.

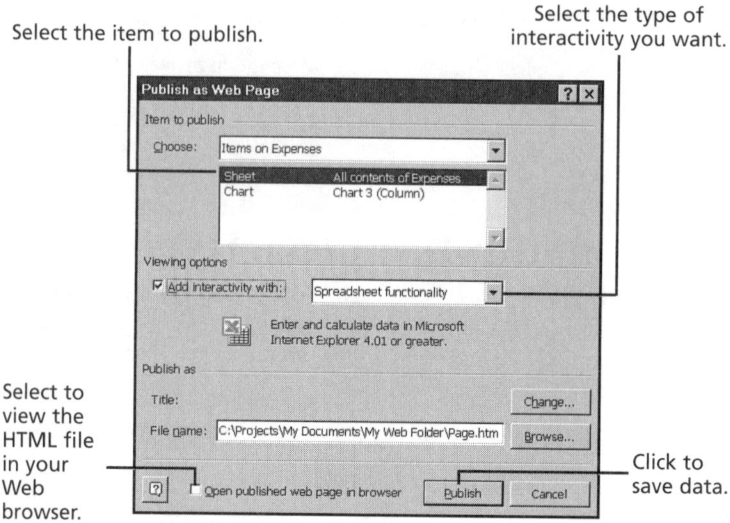

Select the item to publish.

Select the type of interactivity you want.

Select to view the HTML file in your Web browser.

Click to save data.

FIGURE 27.4   Using the Publish as Web Page dialog box to publish interactive data.

9. If you want, select Open published web page in browser to launch your Web browser so you can view the HTML file.

10. Click Publish.

CHANGING INTERACTIVE DATA

When a user views your interactive data in his or her Web browser, it will look something like Figure 27.5.

To change any of the data, just click in a cell, type new data, and press Enter or use an arrow key to move to another cell. You can also use the buttons on the Web Components toolbar as needed. (See Table 27.1.) If you display the Property toolbox, you can change the format of a cell, show or hide data, locate data, change calculations, and control when calculations occur.

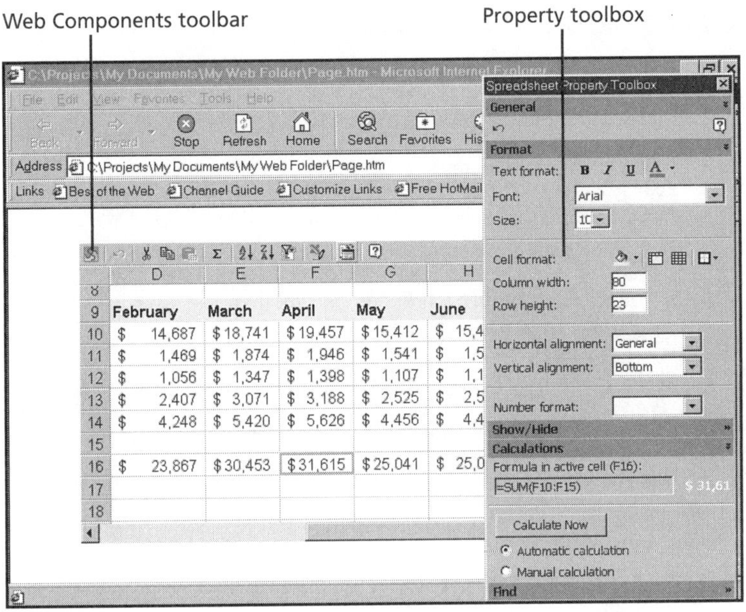

Web Components toolbar   Property toolbox

FIGURE 27.5 How your interactive data looks in a Web browser.

TABLE 27.1 WEB COMPONENTS TOOLBAR

BUTTON	NAME	DESCRIPTION
	Undo	Undo an action
	Cut	Cut data
	Copy	Copy data
	Paste	Paste data
	AutoSum	Create a subtotal
	Sort Ascending	Sort data in ascending order
	Sort Descending	Sort data in descending order
	AutoFilter	Display only selected data
	Export to Excel	Export the data to Excel
	Property Toolbox	Display the Property toolbox
	Help	Display Help

REPUBLISHING YOUR DATA

After your data has been published, follow these steps to update it:

1. Open the original workbook.

2. Make changes as needed.

3. Open the File menu and select Save as Web Page. The Save as Web Page dialog box appears.

4. If you saved the entire workbook before, then just click Save. Otherwise, click Publish.

5. Select Previously Published Items from the Choose list.

6. Choose the item you want to republish from those listed.

7. Make any other changes as needed, then click Publish.

ADDING HYPERLINKS TO A WORKSHEET

A hyperlink is a bit of text or a graphic that, when clicked, takes the user to a Web page, to a file on your hard disk, or to a file on a local network. You can also add a hyperlink to another sheet in the workbook if you like. To add a hyperlink, follow these steps:

1. Select the text or graphic you want to use for the link.

2. Click the Insert Hyperlink button on the Standard toolbar.

3. If asked, make sure you save your workbook. The Insert Hyperlink dialog box appears, as shown in Figure 27.6.

4. Perform one of the following:

> **To link to a file or Web page.** Enter the address of the Web page or file to which you want to link in the Type the file or Web page name text box, or click the File or Web Page button to select it from a dialog box. You can also click Recent Files or Browsed Pages to select it from a list. If you want to click to a bookmark within a Web page, select the page first, then click the Bookmark button, and select the bookmark you want to use.

To link to a location within the workbook. Click the Place in This Document button in the Places bar. Then enter the cell address in the Type the cell reference text box, or select it from the Or select a place in this document list.

To create a link to a new workbook. Click the Create New Document button in the Places bar. Then type a name for the document in the Name of new document text box. To save the workbook in a directory other than the one shown, click the Browse button and select the directory you want to use.

To create a link to an email address (so that when clicked, the link will open your email program, display a message window, and automatically address the email message), click the E-Mail Address button in the Places bar. Then type the email address you want to link to in the E-mail address text box, or select one from the Recently used email addresses list. If you want to enter a subject for the message, type one in the Subject text box.

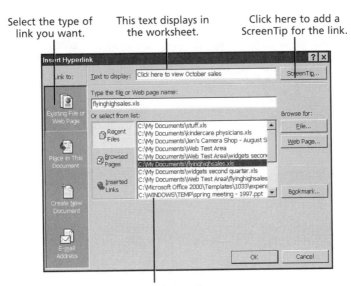

FIGURE 27.6   Insert a hyperlink in a workbook.

5. To display a ScreenTip when the mouse pointer rests on the hyperlink, click ScreenTip, and enter the description you want to display. Click OK.

6. Click OK. The text in the cell you selected becomes blue and underlined.

When you move the mouse pointer over this link, it changes to a hand. Next to the hand, you can see the address of the link. Click the link, and you're jumped to the appropriate worksheet, Web page, file, or email program. The text of the link changes to purple to indicate that you have used the link.

If you need to change the text for a link later on, or change the item that the link points to, right-click link, and select Hyperlink from the shortcut menu. Then select Edit Hyperlink. The Edit Hyperlink dialog box appears. Make your changes and click OK. To delete the link, right-click, select Hyperlink, then select Remove Link from the shortcut menu.

In this lesson, you learned how to save workbook files to an FTP site, how to publish your workbook data, and to add hyperlinks. In the next lesson, you'll learn how to turn your worksheet into a database.

LESSON 28

WORKING WITH A DATABASE

In this lesson, you will learn some database basics and how to create your own database.

DATABASE BASICS

A database is a tool used for storing, organizing, and retrieving information. For example, if you want to save the names and addresses of all the people on your holiday card list, you can create a database and then save the following information for each person: first name, last name, street number, and so on. Each piece of information is entered into a separate field (cell) in the list. All the fields for one person in the list make a record.

In Excel, a cell is a *field*, and a row of field entries makes a *record*. The column labels in the list are called *field names*. Figure 28.1 shows a database and its component parts.

> **Database or Data List?** Excel has simplified the database operations by treating the database as a simple list of data. You enter the database information just like you would enter data into a worksheet. When you select a command from the Data menu, Excel recognizes the list as a database.

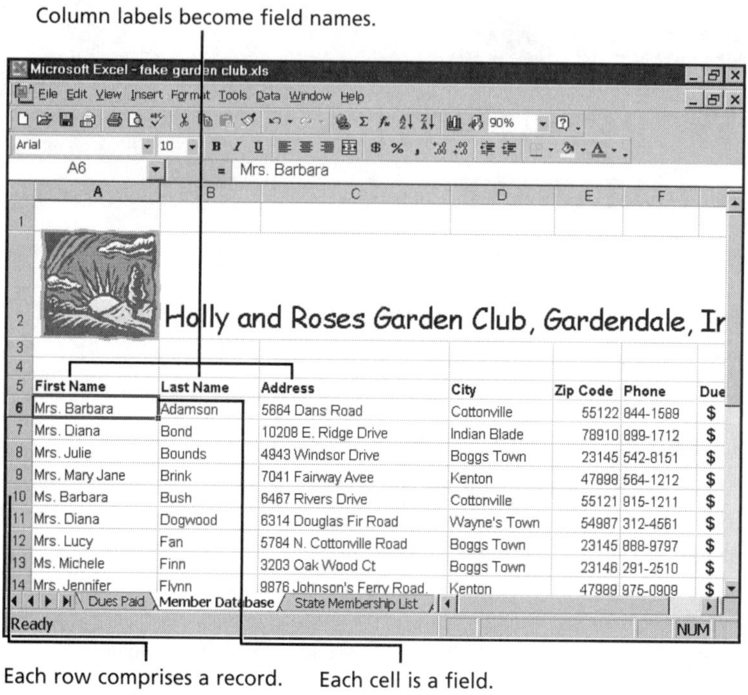

Column labels become field names.

Each row comprises a record.   Each cell is a field.

FIGURE 28.1   The parts of a database.

You must observe the following rules when you enter information into your database:

- **Field Names.** You must enter field names in the first row of the database. For example, you might type **First Name** for the column that will hold first names, and you might type **Last Name** for the column that will hold last names. *Do not skip a row between the field names row and the first record.*

- **Records.** Each record must be in a separate row, and there cannot be any empty rows between records.

- **Same Type.** The cells in a given column must contain information of the same type. For example, if you have a zip code column, all cells in that column must contain a zip code, and not some other kind of data. A cell can be left blank if a particular column does not apply to that record.

- **Calculations.** You can create a calculated field that uses information from another field of the same record and produces a
  result. For example, if you have a column called "Sales
  Amount," you could use a formula to create the values in a column called "Sales Commission." (To do so, enter a formula, as
  explained in Lesson 18.)

> **Record Numbering**   You might want to add a column
> that numbers the records. The record number is likely
> to be the only thing about the record that won't be
> repeated in another record, and having a unique field
> could come in handy in searching and sorting complex
> databases. Also, if the records are sorted incorrectly,
> you can use the numbered column to restore the
> records to their original order.

PLANNING A DATABASE

Before you create your database, you should ask yourself these questions:

- **What are the fields that make up an individual record?** If
  you are creating the database to take the place of an existing
  form (a Rolodex card, information sheet, or address list), use
  that form to determine which fields you need.

- **Which types of data might you want to sort by?** If you want
  to sort by last name, make sure that last name is stored in its
  own field, and not combined with the first name in a single field.
  If you want to sort by city, phone number, or ZIP code, make
  sure that each of these is stored in its own field.

- **Which types of data might you want to search for?** If you
  want to search for all contacts who work in a particular sales
  area, make sure you place the name of the sales area for which
  each person works in its own field.

- **What is the most often referenced field in the database?** This
  field should be placed in the first column.

- **What is the longest entry in each column?** Use this information to set the column widths. (Or you can make your entries and then use Format, Column, AutoFit Selection to have Excel adjust the column widths.)

CREATING A DATABASE

To create a database, you don't have to use any special commands. All you do is enter data into the cells as you would enter data on any worksheet. However, as you enter data, you must follow these guidelines:

- **Enter field names in the top row of the database.** Enter the first record just below this field name row (the row with column labels).

- **Type field entries into each cell in a single row to create a record.** (You can leave a field blank, but you may run into problems later when you sort the database—that is, if you sort the database by that particular field.)

- **Do not leave an empty row between the field names and the records or between any records.**

- **If you want to enter street numbers with the street names at the beginning of the field (such as 155 State Street), start the entry with an apostrophe** so that Excel interprets the entry as text instead of as a value. However, note that if you want to enter, for example, One Washington Square Suite 600, you don't need the apostrophe because it begins with text.

- **Keep the records on one worksheet.** You cannot have a database that spans several worksheets.

 Forget Someone?   To add records to a database, either add the rows above the last row in the database (see Lesson 13, "Inserting and Removing Cells, Rows, and Columns") or select the Data, Form command and enter the additional records using the data form.

USING DATA FORMS TO ADD, EDIT, OR DELETE RECORDS

Data forms are like index cards: there is one data form for each record in the database, as shown in Figure 28.2. You may find it easier to flip through these data form "cards" and edit entries than to edit them as worksheet data. To edit your database using a data form, perform the following steps:

1. Open the Data menu and select Form. You will see a data form that contains the first record in the database (see Figure 28.2).

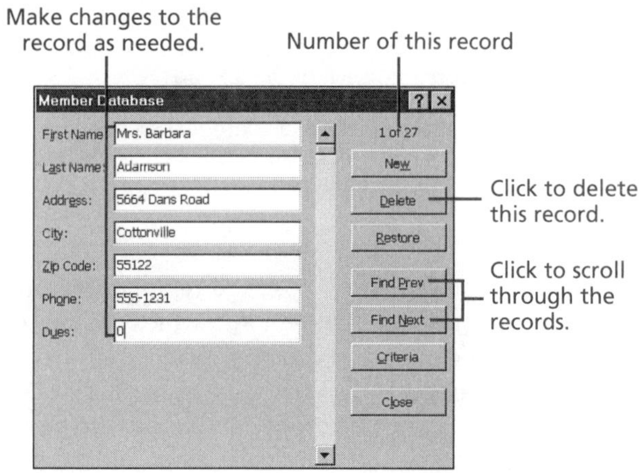

FIGURE **28.2**   The data form.

2. The number of the current record appears in the upper-right corner of the form. Flip to the form you want to edit by using the scrollbar, pressing the up or down arrow key, or clicking Find Prev or Find Next.

3. To edit an entry in a record, tab to the text box that contains the entry and type your correction.

4. To delete the current record, click Delete.

5. Repeat steps 2–4 to change as many records as needed.

6. Click the Close button when you're done using the data form.

Come Back!   You can restore field data to what it was before you changed it—provided you haven't changed to a different record. To do so, click the Restore button. After you move on to a different record, you'll just have to retype the field data.

You can also use the data form to add records to the database, as described here:

1. Open the Data menu and choose Form to display the data form.

2. Click the New button.

3. Type an entry into each of the text boxes.

4. Repeat steps 2 and 3 to add additional records.

5. When you finish adding records, click Close.

Automatic Entry   Use the Template Wizard to create a worksheet template into which you can enter some of the data that you later want to save in a database. For example, you could create a sales worksheet and then link it to a client database so you can save information on the items each client purchases. Just open the Data menu and select Template Wizard. (If you don't see this command, you need to install the Template Wizard add-in.) The Template Wizard walks you step by step through linking cells in the template to fields in a database.

In this lesson, you learned about database basics and how to create a database. In the next lesson, you will learn how to sort the database and find individual records.

Lesson 29

Finding and Sorting Data in a Database

In this lesson, you will learn how to sort a database and how to find individual records.

Finding Data with a Data Form

To find records in a database, you use the Criteria Form, in which you tell Excel the specific information or range of information you want to find— the *criteria*. You can look for something specific, such as a person with the last name Brown, or you can look for a condition that must be evaluated, such as all records containing sales amounts less than $1,000. Table 29.1 shows the operators you can use for comparisons.

TABLE 29.1   EXCEL'S COMPARISON OPERATORS

OPERATOR	MEANING
=	Equal to
>	Greater than
<	Less than
≥	Greater than or equal to
≤	Less than or equal to
≠	Not equal to

For example, if you wanted to search for records containing sales amounts greater than $1,000, you would enter **>1000** in the Sales field on the criteria form.

When specifying criteria, you can also use the following wildcards (characters used to represent information you don't know, or information that is common to many records) when specifying criteria:

?   Represents a single character

*   Represents multiple characters

For example, in the Last Name field, you could type **M*** to find everyone whose last name begins with an M. To find everyone whose three-digit department code has 10 as the last two digits, you could type **?10**.

To find individual records in a database:

1. Open the Data menu and select Form. The Data Form dialog box appears.

2. Click the Criteria button, and the Criteria Form shown in Figure 29.1 appears.

FIGURE 29.1   Selecting search criteria.

3. Type the criteria you would like to use in the appropriate fields. Use only the fields you want to search. For example, if you want to find all Texans whose last names start with B, type **TX** in the State field, type **B*** in the Last Name field, and leave the other fields blank.

4. Select Find Next or Find Prev to look through the list of matching records.

5. When you finish reviewing records, click Close.

Only Real Data, Please   The data field that you are searching cannot be a calculated field. Excel finds only real (typed in) values.

SORTING DATA IN A DATABASE

To sort data in a database, first decide which field to sort by. For example, an address database could be sorted by Last Name or by City (or it could be sorted by Last Name within City within State). Each of these sort fields is considered a *key*.

You can use up to three keys when sorting your database. The first key in the preceding example would be State, the second would be City, and the third would be Last Name. In other words, all the records would be sorted by state. Then within a state, they would be sorted in order by city. And within each city, the names would be sorted in alphabetical order by last name. You can sort your database in ascending or descending order.

Sort Orders   *Ascending* order sorts records from beginning to end, for example from A to Z or 1 to 100. (Records with a blank sort field appear in front of other records.) *Descending* order sorts records the opposite way, from Z to A or from 100 to 1.

For the Record   When you select the database range you want to sort, make sure you include all of the records, but do not include the column labels (field names). If you select the column labels row by accident, then make sure you select the option, Header row (see Figure 29.2), or it will be sorted along with all the other rows and may not remain at the top of your database.

Follow these steps to sort your database:

1. Select the area to be sorted. To sort the entire data list, you can just click any cell in the list.

2. Open the Data menu and choose Sort. The Sort dialog box shown in Figure 29.2 appears.

Select as many as three sorting criteria.

Sort	? X
Sort by	
City ▼	⊙ Ascending ○ Descending
Then by	
Zip Code ▼	⊙ Ascending ○ Descending
Then by	
Last Name ▼	⊙ Ascending ○ Descending
My list has	
⊙ Header row ○ No header row	
Options...	OK Cancel

Choose whether your list contains column labels.

FIGURE 29.2   Selecting the sort criteria.

3. Use the Sort by drop-down list to select the first field you want to sort by and click Ascending or Descending to specify a sort order.

4. To sort by one or two additional fields, select fields from the first and second Then by drop-down lists and choose sort order buttons for each. To remove a sort criteria from a previous sort attempt, open its list box and select (none).

5. Click OK or press Enter.

Undoing a Sort   If the sorting operation does not turn out as planned, you can undo the sort by clicking Undo. To sort even more safely, you might also consider saving a copy of your database file under a different name before sorting. That way, if anything goes wrong, you can open your original database file.

To quickly sort your database by a single field, simply click a cell in that column and click the Sort Ascending or Sort Descending button on the Standard toolbar.

NARROWING YOUR LIST WITH AUTOFILTER

AutoFilter allows you to easily display only a select group of records in your database. For example, you can display the records for only those people who live in Boston. Here's how you use AutoFilter:

1. Click any cell in the database.

2. Open the Data menu, select Filter, and then select AutoFilter. Excel displays drop-down list arrow buttons inside each of the heading cells.

3. Click the drop-down arrow for the field you want to use to filter the list. For example, if you want to display records for those people living in Boston, click the City cell's drop-down arrow. A drop-down list appears, as shown in Figure 29.3. This list shows all the entries in the column.

4. Select the entry you want to use to narrow your list. You can use the arrow keys to scroll through the list, or you can type the first character in the entry's name to quickly move to it. Press Enter or click the entry. For example, if you choose Boston, Excel filters the list so that only the records for people living in Boston appear.

> **Undoing a List**   To return to the full list, open the drop-down list you originally opened (it's marked with a blue arrow) and choose (All). Or, you can remove the AutoFilter drop-down arrows by selecting Data, Filter, AutoFilter.

Open the list and select the type of record you want displayed.

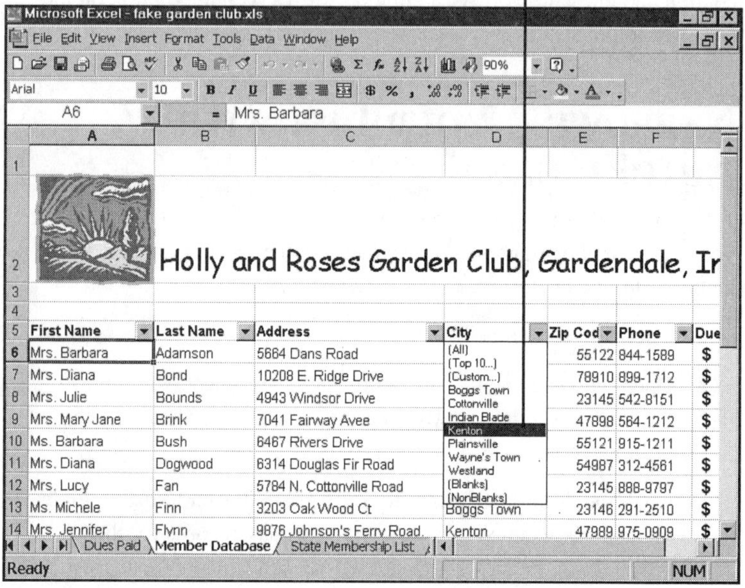

FIGURE 29.3   AutoFilter lets you narrow your list.

The Custom option in the AutoFilter drop-down list lets you apply two criteria values within the current column, or use comparison operators And and Or. To use the Custom option, click the drop-down list button for the field you want to filter and select Custom. Excel displays the Custom AutoFilter dialog box. Enter your preferences and click OK to filter your data.

The Top 10 option enables you to display all rows that contain the highest or lowest (best or worst) items in a list. For example, you could select the top 10 percent (such as the top 10 percent of sales revenues) or you could select the top 10 values in your total list (such as the top 10 sales revenues). Choose the Top 10 option in the AutoFilter drop-down list, enter your preferences in the Top 10 AutoFilter dialog box, and then click OK to filter your data.

The Blanks option enables you to display all the rows that contain no data in a particular column. The NonBlanks option works the opposite way, displaying only those rows that actually contain data in the selected column.

Look It Up!   With the Lookup Wizard, you can locate one piece of information by looking up something else. For example, if you have a sales database, you could find the name of the salesperson who sold a particular item. To use the Lookup Wizard, open the Tools menu, select Wizard, and select Lookup. (If you don't see the command, you will need to install the Lookup Wizard add-in first.)

In this lesson, you learned how to find individual records and how to sort and filter your database. In the next lesson, you will learn how to add graphics and other objects to your worksheets.

LESSON 30

ADDING GRAPHICS AND OTHER OBJECTS TO WORKSHEETS

In this lesson, you will learn how to add graphic objects to your work-sheets.

WORKING WITH GRAPHIC OBJECTS

Excel comes with several tools that enable you to add graphic objects to your workbooks and charts. You can add a graphic object created in another program, you can add clip art (predrawn art that comes with Excel and other programs), or you can draw your own graphic objects using the Drawing toolbar.

> **Graphic Object** A *graphic object* is anything in your worksheet that isn't data. Graphic objects include things you can draw (such as ovals and rectangles), text boxes, charts, and clip art.

INSERTING CLIP ART

Excel comes with a nice collection of clip art pictures that you can use to enhance your worksheet. To insert a picture, follow these steps:

More, More! If you're upgrading from a previous version of Excel, you'll be glad to learn that the Gallery contains more images than before, and that it is much easier to use.

1. Select the cell in which you want the upper-left corner of the picture placed.

2. Open the Insert menu, choose Picture, and choose Clip Art. The Insert ClipArt dialog box appears, as shown in Figure 30.1.

3. If necessary, click the Pictures tab. Then select a category from those listed. For example, click Business.

Click here to return to
the previous page.

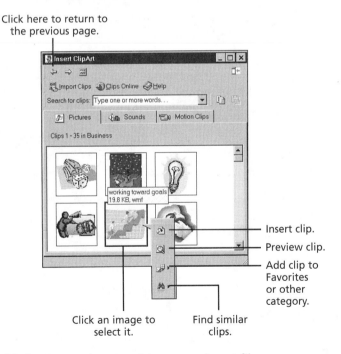

Insert clip.

Preview clip.

Add clip to Favorites or other category.

Click an image to select it.

Find similar clips.

FIGURE 30.1   You can insert a picture or a clip art file.

4. Click an image to select it. A shortcut menu appears as seen in Figure 30.1.

 Find That Clip!   To find a piece of clip art quickly, type a few keywords into the Search for clips text box. For example, you might type **win** to find an image that depicts victory.

5. Select an option from the shortcut menu:

Insert clip. This option inserts the clip art image into your worksheet.

Preview clip. Choose this option to display the image in a small window, slightly bigger than it's displayed in the dialog box.

Add clip to Favorites or other category. Click here and select the category in which you want this image copied. In this way, you can organize the Clip Art Gallery the way you like.

Find similar clips. This option searches the Gallery for clip art images that are similar to the one you selected, based on the keywords that were used to describe it.

You can move the picture by dragging it. To resize the picture, click on it first to select it, and then drag one of its handles (the small squares that appear around the image when it's selected). Drag a corner handle to change both the width and height proportionally. Drag a side handle to change only the width, or drag a top or bottom handle to change only the height.

ADDING YOUR OWN CLIP ART, VIDEO CLIPS, OR SOUND CLIPS TO THE GALLERY

Excel allows you to organize your clip art images, sound clips, and video clips in its Clip Gallery. Once you import a file into the Gallery, you can insert it into any Microsoft Office document, including an Excel work-book, Word document, or PowerPoint presentation. Follow these steps to import a file into the Gallery:

1. Open the Insert menu, select Picture, and select Clip Art.

2. Click the tab for the type of file you want to import. For example, to import a video clip, click the Motion Clips tab.

3. Click Import Clips. The Add clip to Clip Gallery dialog box appears.

4. Change to the folder that contains the file you want to import and select the file from the list.

5. Select an option:

   Copy into Clip Gallery. Copies the file into the Clip Gallery folder.

   Move into Clip Gallery. Moves the file into the Clip Gallery folder.

   Let Clip Gallery find this clip in its current folder or volume. Indexes the file without copying or moving it.

6. Click Import. The Clip Properties dialog box appears, as shown in Figure 30.2.

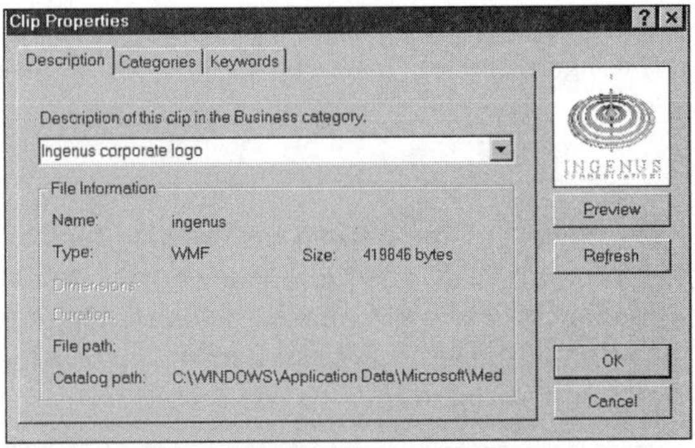

FIGURE 30.2   Importing an image into the Gallery.

7. Type a description for the clip in the text box.

8. Click the Categories tab and select the category or categories in which you want the clip to appear.

Can't Find an Appropriate Category? You can create a new category if you want, by clicking New Category, entering a name, and clicking OK.

9. Click the Keywords tab. To add a keyword to describe the clip, click New Keyword. Then type the keyword you want to add, and click OK. For example, you might add the keywords **happy**, **people**, and **winning**.

10. Click OK, and the clip is added to the Gallery.

To insert the clip into a worksheet, follow the same basic steps that you did to insert clip art: open the Insert menu, select Picture, and select Clip Art. Click the tab for the type of clip you want to insert, and then click the category to which it belongs. Select the clip you want and click Insert clip to import it into your worksheet.

DRAWING YOUR OWN PICTURES

You can add arrows, text boxes, and other objects to your worksheets or your charts by using the Drawing toolbar. Table 30.1 lists the tools on the Drawing toolbar.

New to You If you've used the Drawing toolbar in the previous version of Excel, you won't be too surprised by how it works. However, you should note the addition of the Insert Clip Art button, which allows you to insert clip art quickly and simply.

TABLE 30.1   TOOLS ON THE DRAWING TOOLBAR

TOOL	NAME	DESCRIPTION
Draw ▾	Draw	Contains commands for grouping, rotating, and aligning objects
	Select Objects	Enables you to select an object
	Free Rotate	Rotates an object
AutoShapes ▾	AutoShapes	Offers tools with which you can create lots of predrawn shapes, such as arrows, stars, and callouts
	Line	Draws a curved or straight line
	Arrow	Draws an arrow
	Rectangle	Draws a square or a rectangle
	Oval	Draws a circle or an oval
	Text Box	Adds text (in a moveable box) to a worksheet or chart
	Insert WordArt	Adds shaped text
	Insert Clip Art	Adds a piece of clip art to the worksheet
	Fill Color	Changes the color of a selected object
	Line Color	Changes the color of an object's outline
	Font Color	Changes the color of text
	Line Style	Changes the style of a line object

continues

TABLE 30.1   CONTINUED

TOOL	NAME	DESCRIPTION
	Dash Style	Changes the default dash style
	Arrow Style	Changes the style of an arrow object
	Shadow	Adds a shadow to an object
	3D	Makes an object appear 3D

To use any of the tools on the Drawing toolbar, click the button, and then click and drag within the worksheet to create the shape. For example, to create a text box, click the Text Box button. Then click in the worksheet or chart where you want to place the upper-left corner of the text box, and drag downward and to the right to create the text box. Type your message into the box, and then click within the worksheet to deselect the text box.

When you click on a drawn object, handles appear around it to show that it's selected. Once it's selected, you can resize the object by dragging one of its handles outward (to make it bigger) or inward (to make it smaller). You can move an object by dragging it.

Group Them Together   Excel lets you group objects together so you can move, resize, and format them as a single unit. Press and hold the Shift key and click each object you want to group. Then click the Draw button and select Group.

In this lesson, you learned how to add graphic objects and other objects to your worksheets and charts. You also learned how to use Excel's drawing tools to enhance the appearance of worksheets and charts.

INDEX